THE SECOND GREATEST INVENTION

By Eleanor Clymer

THE SECOND GREATEST INVENTION
THE BIG PILE OF DIRT
MY BROTHER STEVIE
WHEELS
SEARCH FOR A LIVING FOSSIL

THE SECOND GREATEST INVENTION
Search for the First Farmers

by ELEANOR CLYMER

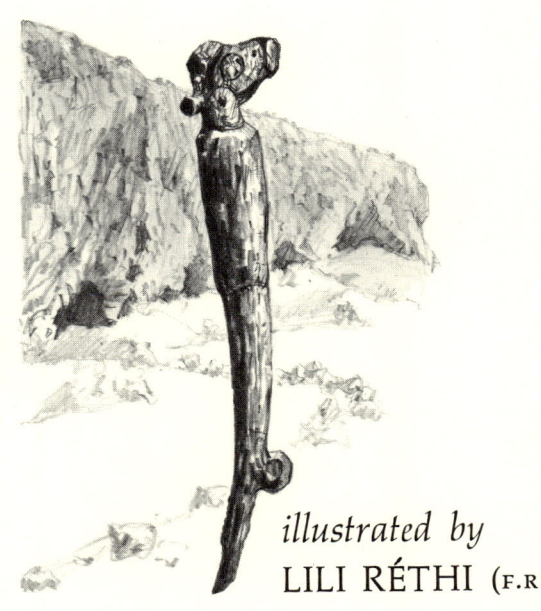

illustrated by
LILI RÉTHI (F.R.S.A.)

224863

HOLT, RINEHART AND WINSTON
NEW YORK   CHICAGO   SAN FRANCISCO

For Kinsey

Text Copyright © 1969 by Eleanor Clymer.
Illustrations Copyright © 1969 by Holt, Rinehart
and Winston, Inc.
All rights reserved, including the right to reproduce
this book or portions thereof in any form.
Published simultaneously in Canada by Holt, Rinehart
and Winston of Canada, Limited.
SBN:03-072390-6
Library of Congress Catalog Card Number: 69-10240
Printed in the United States of America
First Edition

Contents

    Preface   1
1. The Mysterious Stones   6
2. Stone Age Man in Europe   15
3. Egypt   25
4. The Near East   39
5. New Ways in Archaeology   55
6. Jarmo   63
7. The Natufians   71
8. The Great Change Begins   79
9. Animals and Plants Change   93
10. People Change   103
    Index   115

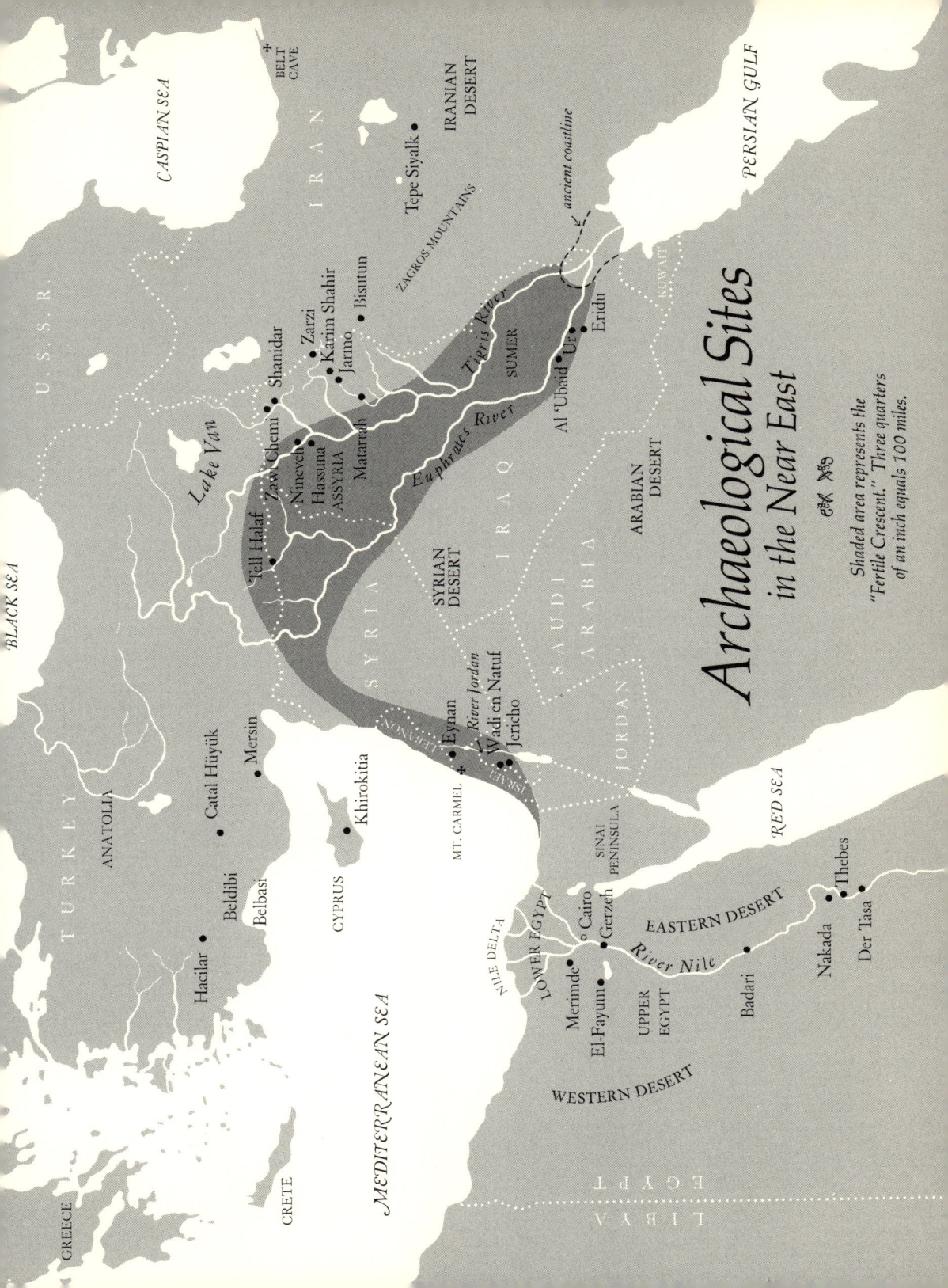

Archaeological Sites in the Near East

Shaded area represents the "Fertile Crescent." Three quarters of an inch equals 100 miles.

Preface

People love mysteries. If there is anything hidden or secret, or the least bit mysterious, they've got to find out about it. You know how it is yourself. If there is a big sealed package, you want to know what's inside. If you hear a few words, or a rumor, you've got to know the whole story.

Those are very ordinary examples. There are plenty of more exciting ones. People want to know what's under the ocean, what makes thunder, why a teakettle boils.

They want to know what happened in the past: who won a battle, who shot a president, how the West was settled.

People want to know even more difficult things: how the earth was made, how life began, where man himself came from, how he became what he is today.

They want so much to know that they work like anything to find out. Scientists labor in the laboratory. Historians pore over books in the library. Explorers toil through deserts and ice fields and jungles to find out what's there. They give all kinds of good reasons. They say that the more we can learn the better our lives will be or something like that. This may indeed be the result of much of their exertion. It isn't necessarily the cause. The fact is, people just can't resist a mystery. They've got to know.

There was a man who was asked why he wanted to climb Mount Everest, the world's highest mountain. He said, "Because it's there." That may have been the most honest answer ever given. If something is there, man has to find out about it. At least he has to figure out some sort of explanation.

And of all mysterious subjects, man himself is the greatest teaser.

Where did he come from? Why is he so unlike all others in the animal kingdom? Most interesting of all, how did man make himself the boss of the world, ruling all other species, so that by now he really feels the world belongs to him!

For a long time there were no answers to these questions. All the ancient people, it is true, had stories of the Creation. The Greeks said the world was made and ruled by some gods who lived on top of Mount Olympus. The most ancient myth of the Egyptians said that there was a watery, dark nothingness, with just one little island in the middle of it, and on that island was the god Atum, who created all the rest of the universe including man. The Bible tells how Jehovah made the earth and all the animals, and then man, and placed man in charge of everything else. For a long time there was no other information about the origin of things.

It was not until about 250 years ago that scientists, with their insatiable curiosity, began systematically to dig into the earth itself, and to find clues to the beginnings of man. And in those 250 years they learned a good deal. They found that man started out as a puny race, a few primitive groups scattered throughout Africa, competing with the other animals for whatever food they could scavenge. But they wouldn't have been able to compete if they hadn't made a great invention—man's first and greatest invention: tools.

Those apelike creatures found that sharp stones could be used as tools and weapons, to kill game, cut up meat, and fight enemies. First they used just cracked pebbles. Then they learned to shape their stones more skillfully.

This meant that our ancestors could survive, and they did. For a million years or more they were hunters and gatherers of berries, roots, snails, tortoises, and whatever else they could find. They became cleverer. Their brains developed. They spread from Africa to Europe and Asia, getting more human all the time. They kept improving on their great invention, making better tools all the time.

But a big mystery remained. There was a tremendous gap between those ancient hunters and present-day man. Hunters spend nearly all their time hunting. Modern man builds cities, paints pictures, runs railroads, flies planes. He does all the thousands of things that add up to civilization. What is

Pebble tool from East Africa.

the secret of his success? Somehow he must be freed from the endless work of food-getting. Somebody must provide the necessary food for all the people who do all this other work. Who does it? Farmers.

Farmers produce food. That is the big difference. Food production gave mankind the big push forward that it needed. Food production was man's second greatest invention.

But how did this start? People have been speculating about it for thousands of years. There are myths, folk memories and stories about this too.

The story we know best is from the Bible. It tells how Adam and Eve were placed in a lovely garden called Eden— the name comes from a Hebrew word meaning delight or pleasure. Then they gained some forbidden knowledge by eating the fruit of a certain tree. This made Jehovah very angry, and he cast them forth, saying, "Thou shalt eat of the herb of the field; in the sweat of thy face shalt thou eat bread."

So Man became a farmer. But this doesn't give all the facts. The story is very sketchy, though beautiful. Where did men become farmers? Who were they? How did they learn what to do? All this remained a mystery, though there was a feeling that Eden must have been somewhere in Mesopotamia.

It wasn't until scientists, with their insatiable curiosity, went digging in all the corners of the earth, that we found the evidence of the truth of some of these stories, and clues to what really happened.

The scientists were archaeologists, men and women who study the relics that ancient people leave behind, and from them figure out how those people lived.

By now, archaeologists have found enough evidence to give us a picture of the way people first learned to plant seeds and gather crops and herd animals.

It is a fascinating story. And just as fascinating is the story of the archaeologists themselves—who they were, what they did, and how they interpreted the bits of bones and broken jars they found. That is what this book is about. I hope it will satisfy some of *your* insatiable curiosity.

1 ⚜ The Mysterious Stones

How did anybody know where to begin looking for clues to ancient man? The answer is, they didn't. Only a couple of hundred years ago, very few people even suspected there was such a thing.

As recently as that, a great many people in Europe believed that the Bible story of creation was literally true. (Some people today still do. Others believe it must be interpreted to fit in with present knowledge.) It used to be thought that the earth had been created in a week, in 4004 B.C. It was further believed that not long after the Creation, the people on earth became so wicked that God caused every living thing to perish in a great flood, except for Noah and his family and the animals in the Ark. And so all the people and animals currently living on earth must have descended from those passengers.

But for a long time evidence had been appearing that perhaps there was more to the story than that.

Every so often, through the ages, certain strangely shaped

pieces of stone had been found. Now stone is about the commonest thing there is. The whole earth is made of it. Pieces break off, and big rocks, little pebbles are everywhere. Some are cracked and chipped, some are worn smooth by wind and water.

But these particular stones didn't look natural. They looked as if they had been deliberately shaped by human hands. Greek and Roman farmers, plowing their fields, or workmen digging ditches or cellars or gravel pits, used to find them. But who could have made them? Nobody could imagine.

Some ancient Greeks used to say that these stones had fallen from the sky. They were thunderbolts, hurled to earth during a storm by Zeus, the god of thunder!

A few of the ancient Greeks and Romans did realize that man had not always been civilized. Herodotus, a Greek historian who lived from about 485 to 430 B.C., and who traveled all over the ancient world, wrote about the wild tribes he met in his travels. He described the Scythians, who hunted on horseback and shot stone-tipped arrows.

The Roman poet Lucretius, in the first century B.C., wrote long poems describing how the first men fought with fists, or branches, or stones, and then later with brass and iron. But this was mostly imagination, though it was a pretty good guess, and it didn't explain who left the "thunderbolts."

Centuries passed. The Middle Ages passed, and in fifteenth-

A "thunderbolt."

century Europe the Renaissance was beginning. The Greeks and Romans had been forgotten for a long time, but now they were being remembered again. Their ancient books were found hidden away in monasteries and libraries, and the ruins of their buildings and sculptures were discovered, still standing, or buried in the earth. Many people rushed to Italy and Greece to dig for these ancient things, or "antiquities."

This was how archaeology began. At first it was simply the search for ancient works of art which wealthy people wanted to decorate their houses. But soon, archaeologists began to find other ancient things, not so beautiful but very interesting—and puzzling.

Here and there, in Italy, France, Belgium, England, those curiously chipped stones kept turning up. They were still being called "thunderbolts." Some scholars tried to make sense out of this. Since they didn't believe in Zeus any more, they said the stones were a kind of solidified lightning!

There were others however who insisted they must have been made by men. About this time America was discovered and explored. When the Indians were found using stone tools very much like the "thunderbolts," it didn't seem so impossible after all. But what men could ever have used them in Europe? Nobody knew.

Then some very disturbing discoveries were made. Strange fossilized animal bones had been found buried deep in the earth—bones of elephants and rhinoceroses and enormous

8

bears. These finds were disturbing because they upset many people's ideas about the age of the earth. The new science of geology was growing up. Students of natural history saw that wind and water were wearing away the rocks in some places, and building them up in others.

This was a very slow process. At the rate at which it was happening, it must surely have taken more than 6,000 years for the earth to be formed. Some people bravely estimated 100,000 years! (We know now that it took 4½ *billion!*) Still it was clear that these animals must have lived very, very long ago, long before the Flood.

Then, to make things more confusing, some of those flint "thunderbolts" and even some human bones were found together with animal fossils. This seemed to mean that people too must have lived in that far distant past.

There were many excited arguments about all this. Some said it was impossible for men to have lived so long before the Flood. Some said there must have been a series of floods or catastrophes.

But how could elephants and giant bears and other strange beasts have lived in England and France and Germany? By 1840 an explanation was found for this mystery.

A Swiss scientist named Louis Agassiz had been studying the glaciers, those enormous rivers of ice that flow down the mountains of Switzerland. He proved that many thousands of years ago the glaciers had been much larger, in fact all of

Part of the Greenland icecap. Much of Europe must have looked like this at the end of the Ice Age.

the northern half of Europe had been covered with masses of ice several miles thick! The great elephant (really a mammoth), the cave bear, the woolly rhinoceros were all cold-weather animals that had lived at the edges of the ice fields in those times.

By 1859 scientists had to accept the idea that early men had really existed in Europe long before the beginning of history. They were hunters. For their food they killed the animals of the Ice Age. And the chipped flints in French gravel pits and in English caves were the tools and weapons they had left behind. Archaeologists called them "the men of the Stone Age."

Meanwhile more facts had been coming to light. In England there were mounds of earth here and there across the countryside, known as barrows. The country people used to think they were the graves of giants.

Archaeologists, and in fact anybody who was curious about antiquities, dug into the barrows and found, not giants, but the skeletons of quite normal-sized people. Buried with them were weapons, jewelry, pottery, tools, of strange design. Who were these people? Could they be the Druids whom Julius Caesar wrote about, or some of the barbarian tribes he found when he conquered Britain? There was no way to tell.

Denmark too had a great many barrows, and also many peat bogs. A peat bog is a place that was once a swamp and is gradually drying up. But the ground is still damp and spongy. The country people for years had cut blocks of peat to use for fuel, and as they dug they found odd things buried in the peat—bronze and iron swords, cups, armor, and jew-

Chipped flint, side and front view. St. Acheul, France.

elry. And deeper down, there were things made of stone. So ancient man had lived here too!

But these stone objects were not crudely chipped like the "thunderbolts" from the French riverbeds and the English caves. They were stone axes, cups, bowls, beautifully ground and polished.

The Danes were much interested in these things. A number of professors and historians felt there should be a national museum to display them, so that people could see what their forebears had done. People began sending in hundreds of specimens, and they were piling up in the storeroom of the National Library in Copenhagen.

In 1816, a young Dane named Christian Jurgensen Thomsen had been given the job of organizing the museum. But the specimens were all jumbled together. They had to be classified. As there was no system of classification, he invented one. He arranged the objects in three groups—iron, bronze, and stone. He studied them and decided that the stone objects must be the oldest, the bronzes were next, and the iron tools and weapons were the most recent. He called this the Three-Age System. It was the first practical method of dating antiquities, and gradually it came to be accepted by other scholars.

But why were the Stone Age tools and vessels from Denmark so different from those of the caves and gravel pits?

When the mystery of the glaciers was cleared up, people

Three axes. Polished stone: Danish; bronze: Turkish; iron: Roman.

realized what this meant. The two kinds of tools belonged to two different periods. The chipped tools were made by an earlier race of men, the ones who hunted the great Ice Age animals. The polished stone tools belonged to people who came later, after the climate had warmed up and the ice had melted away from the northern lands.

The Stone Age would have to be divided into two parts—the Palaeolithic or Old Stone Age, and the Neolithic or New Stone Age.

Years later, a third type of tool would be found: tiny flints, cut into geometrical shapes, set into bone or wood handles. They belonged to a time midway between the Palaeolithic and the Neolithic, a time when the ice was just beginning to melt, forests were starting to grow; the big animals of the Ice Age were gone, and new, smaller animals lived in the forests and the lakes and rivers. This was the Mesolithic, the Middle Stone Age.

Europeans were amazed. Right here, practically under their feet, unknown people had lived. And these people had no connection with Druids or any of the tribes mentioned by Greek and Roman historians. They had lived before history. They were prehistoric.

Where had they come from? How did they look? How did they think and talk and act? Nobody knew. But more evidence was soon forthcoming.

2 ❧ Stone Age Man in Europe

In 1856, in the Neanderthal Valley in Germany, some workmen, digging for limestone, found a skull and some leg and rib bones, deep in a cave. The skull bones were thick, with heavy brow ridges, like those of a gorilla. The leg bones were short and thick and curved. Yet the bones were human, and they were fossilized and very ancient. At last, said some scientists, here is our relative.

It was upsetting to Europeans of the civilized nineteenth century to hear that they had a relative who looked so much like an ape.

However, Neanderthal man was not an ape. He had a good brain inside that thick skull. In time, more of his bones were found all over Europe and the Near East, together with his tools—crude but good hand-axes, scrapers, and points. The nineteenth-century archaeologists knew of no way to figure out how old the bones were, but we now know that Neanderthal men lived from about 85,000 to 45,000 years ago.

They were skillful hunters. They had to be to survive some

of the worst weather the world has ever had—centuries of freezing cold, ice and snow. They hunted the cave bears and mammoths, cutting their meat with stone knives and curing the skins with stone scrapers, probably for clothing. They seem to have had an idea of life after death, for they buried their dead carefully, with weapons or food, as if for a journey, and protected the graves with heavy stones.

Archaeologists have found no trace of them in rocks or earth less than forty-five thousand years old. Either they died out, or were killed off, or perhaps they intermarried with another type of man who came to Europe about that time.

This was Cro-Magnon man, so named after the village in the south of France where his bones were first found. There in a rock shelter, in 1868, the French scientist Édouard Lartet discovered flint tools, animal bones and a number of skeletons. Many more of their remains were found later. These people were tall, well-built, with large skulls and high foreheads. Physically, they were just like modern people.

They had well-made stone tools. Some were made by striking off a long, thin blade from a large piece of flint. Some were beautifully chipped tools of different shapes. They used bone too, to make tools, weapons and jewelry. They left pictures of woolly mammoths and bison and reindeer engraved on pieces of mammoth tusk. It was from such pictures that archaeologists first learned how those animals looked.

These were the people who made the magnificent cave

paintings of animals which would be found later in the nineteenth century. And that meant they had plenty to eat, for only when there is a surplus of food can men spare time and energy for art. It was a time of big game and good hunting, and Cro-Magnon men knew how to hunt in well-organized groups.

Both Neanderthal and Cro-Magnon men belonged to the Old Stone Age or Palaeolithic. But it clarified matters to say that Neanderthal belonged to the Lower, or earlier, Palaeolithic, and Cro-Magnon to the Upper, or later, Palaeolithic. Neither type was a native of Europe. They appeared there, fully developed. When geologists dug into the older rocks, they found no sign of man, but only of animals like dinosaurs or ancient fishes. There was no sign of where they came from, and there was nothing to show that they knew anything about farming. Where were the first farmers?

In 1853, something happened that seemed to cast some light on the problem. It happened that in that year, in Switzerland, the winter had been very dry. Very little snow or rain fell. The water in Lake Zurich was lower than it had ever been before. The farmers who lived beside the lake had never had enough level land, for Switzerland is mainly mountains. Now they had a chance to do something about it. They built stone walls down by the water's edge. They were going to dig up mud from the lake bed to fill in the low places inside the walls. Thus they would gain some extra land.

This system had worked in other years. But this time, near the village of Obermeilen, the farmers ran into trouble. When they began to dig in the shallow water, they found rows of posts driven into the mud about a foot apart. These were not mere sticks, but stout tree trunks ten feet high.

The farmers moved to another spot. There were more posts. The whole bay was filled with them. It was like an underwater forest. Who had done this, and why? Nobody could guess. There was nothing to do but scoop up mud from between the posts.

Then came another surprise. The mud they dug up was full of unexpected things. There were bones, broken pottery, pieces of flint, and masses of burnt wood. Since none of this was of any use to them, they dumped it back into the lake.

But then came some more interesting things—axes of bronze, and flint axes with handles of deer antler. The farmers showed these to the schoolmaster, who was the most educated person in the village, and he realized that these things were very old and might be interesting to scholars.

It happened that not far away in the city of Zurich there was an archaeological club. The members were enthusiastic young men who were interested in antiquities, and the leader was Professor Ferdinand Keller, one of the leading archaeologists of the time. The schoolmaster from Obermeilen sent his specimens to them. The club members rushed to Obermeilen, and got to work.

Some of the young men sorted out the things dredged up by the farmers. Others climbed into boats and floated about on the lake, fishing for anything they could find. Soon there was a large pile of objects of all kinds. There were many knives and axes of polished flint, and, to everyone's surprise, some with wooden handles. This was the first time anybody had realized that wood could be preserved by being soaked in water. In the years to come, much more evidence of this would be found in the peat bogs of Denmark, England, Italy, and Ireland.

But there was more than wood. There were pieces of matting, fish nets, baskets, and even linen cloth, not woven but twined or plaited. Gradually the picture became clear. The posts had been the foundations of a prehistoric village. Parts of the flooring were even found to prove it.

Then classical scholars remembered that the Greek historian Herodotus had written of a Thracian tribe that lived in houses built on piles on a small lake in the Balkan mountains of eastern Europe. Their platforms had been connected with the shore by a wooden causeway. They had kept all their animals, even horses, on the platforms, and their food had consisted mainly of fish. This seemed to be the same kind of village.

At once there was feverish excitement. People came to all the lakes in Switzerland to dig in the shallow waters, and they found that the villages were everywhere.

How a Swiss lake village may have looked.

Quantities of charred wood showed that many of the settlements had been destroyed by fire. But the fire which had no doubt been a catastrophe for the villagers proved a blessing to the archaeologists. The charring had helped to preserve carbonized wheat and barley and flat round cakes of bread. These people had grain! They were farmers!

In addition, there were countless bones of cattle, sheep, goats, pigs and dogs. The villagers were animal husbandmen as well.

They also hunted. This was shown by bones of bear, wolf, beaver, deer, fox, and many smaller animals and birds. And they gathered the wild fruits, for there were carbonized apples and pears, berries and nuts, and seeds of wild plums. The fruits and nuts were native to Switzerland—similar ones still grow there—but the wheat and barley were not. They had been brought from some other place.

There was much fishing gear—cords, hooks, and stones for weights. In one place a canoe was found, hollowed out of a single log.

At first, in their great excitement, the workers pulled their prizes helter-skelter out of the lakes. But they soon found that by digging carefully in the mud they could arrange their finds stratigraphically. The iron tools came from the topmost levels, the bronze ones next, and the stone axes from the bottom. Since these were polished or ground stone, the settlements were pronounced Neolithic, or late Stone Age.

The discovery proved the truth of Thomsen's Three-Age System. And there was more evidence than mere stone and bronze and iron. In each level there was a wealth of other material to show how people lived. For the first time, early man began to seem real.

The best examples of Neolithic life came from the Swiss village of Robenhausen, where the lake shore was one big bed of peat. Buried in the water-logged peat were the inevitable piles, their tops at three different levels, showing where different villages had been built. Between the piles were uncounted objects: stone axes mounted in pieces of antler, flint and bone tools, needles, harpoons, spears, and arrows. There was pottery of all kinds. There were bits of woven cloth and mats, balls of yarn, basketwork. There were grain, peas, beans, lentils, and bones of domestic animals. There was no sign of metal. Robenhausen was all Neolithic.

At last the Neolithic Age was not just a theory but a way of life. People had come to the lake shores, cut down trees to build their platforms, and planted the fields that had been cleared. Then the men went hunting and fishing. The women tilled the fields, ground the grain on stone querns or hand mills, baked the bread in clay-lined ovens. They made pottery, wove cloth and baskets, and perhaps made clothing and blankets out of skins.

Probably the children did their share, for in farming villages children can be very useful. They take care of the cows and sheep and goats, and chase birds away from the grain. They go fishing, gather fruit and nuts, and help carry home the crops. There was plenty to do in the villages, and a large population to do it.

But life was not all peaceful. Many villages showed signs of fire. That could have been accidental, if a spark from an oven set fire to a house and then to the whole village. Or it could have meant an attack by outsiders, shooting flaming arrows into the midst of the houses.

Then the people would flee, taking anything they could carry. Later they would return to rebuild the village, or perhaps the invading group would take over the place.

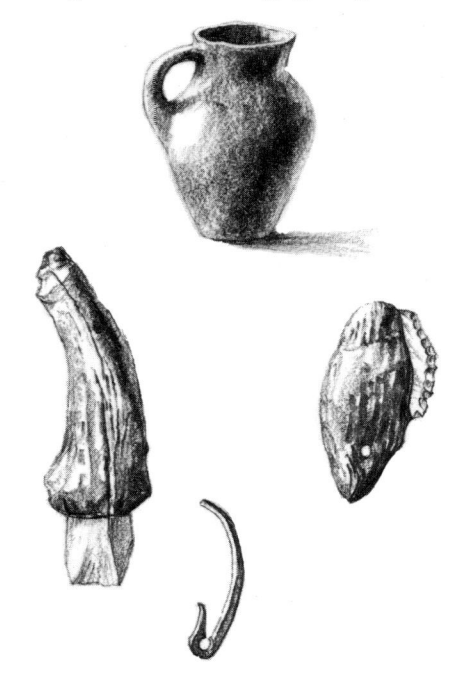

Implements from Swiss lake village (clockwise): chisel in antler handle; pottery jug; flint knife in wooden handle; fishhook from boar's tooth.

But who were the builders of these villages? Were they descendants of the Cro-Magnon reindeer hunters, or of the Neanderthal men of the Old Stone Age? As the archaeologists studied the assemblages, they realized that this was not so. Though the digging went on for more than fifty years, there was no sign of a Palaeolithic settlement underneath the Neolithic villages.

Besides, the Palaeolithic hunters had never shown a tendency to build houses or settle in villages. They knew nothing of making pottery, or polishing stone, or planting seeds or keeping sheep. They never wove cloth or baskets.

The lake-dwellers were newcomers. They had arrived from elsewhere, perhaps looking for new land for their crops like other pioneers, bringing their skills with them. They had brought their flocks and seeds, which were not native to Europe. Probably they had had to fight the native hunters, who were suspicious of them and tried to drive them out by setting fire to their villages.

At last farmers had been found. But farming and herding did not begin in Europe. Regretfully, the workers concluded: "They are not from here." Clues would have to be sought elsewhere. But where?

3 ❧ Egypt

While some archaeologists were discovering Stone Age man in Europe, it happened that others were going eastward, to a land of mystery—to Egypt.

It is true they weren't all going to search for man's beginnings. Some were going to snatch as many antiquities as they could, to take home and sell to the highest bidders.

Others were going out of a sense of romance, or curiosity, or to prove that Bible stories were true.

For thousands of years people had marveled at Egypt, and traveled there to see its wonders. It was a unique country.

Most of it was a desert. (It still is.) But every year the river Nile, pouring down from some mysterious source, rose and flooded the land on either bank, covering it with water and mud, and then flowed on to empty into the Mediterranean Sea. After the flood had passed, that narrow valley was so fertile that it would give two and even three crops a year. In the fifth century B.C. the Greek historian Herodotus described how the Egyptian farmers irrigated their fields. He called Egypt "the gift of the Nile."

As far back as man's memory went, the river had been behaving this way. It was one of the wonders of the world. When there was drought and famine in other places, Egypt had food. That was why the Hebrew people went there, as the Bible tells us, to get grain in time of need. Other nations of the ancient world did the same.

As a result of all this surplus food, Egypt became very rich. A great empire grew up.

The ancient Greeks knew that Egypt's civilization was far older than their own, and they thought Egypt was the birthplace of civilization, perhaps even of life itself. What better place to look for the beginnings of man's history?

But even in the days of the Greeks, much of the ancient history of Egypt had been forgotten.

From the Nile Valley, the land rose in a series of cliffs and terraces to meet the high desert. At the edge of the desert were ancient monuments: pyramids, like man-made mountains; temples and buildings carved out of stone; statues of kings and gods; avenues of sphinxes, and one enormous sphinx. And the walls and the statues were covered with strange picture writing, hieroglyphics that nobody could read. Even when Herodotus visited Egypt, the ancient characters were meaningless to most Egyptians. Only the priests could read them.

For all her greatness, Egypt by the time of Herodotus was past her prime. She was ruled by many different conquerors

—Greeks, Romans, then Arabs. Her ancient buildings were covered by the drifting sands. Through the years travelers continued to come there, braving all sorts of dangers from bandits, disease and the broiling sun. They looked for treasures in the pyramids, or tried to find some mystical meaning in the hieroglyphics, all in vain.

And then something happened that was to unravel the mystery. In 1797 Napoleon went to Egypt. He went because France was at war with the British, and he wanted to cut their trade route to India by taking control of Egypt. But Napoleon liked to do things in a big way. Since he was going there anyway, he would do something the world would long remember. He took along nearly two hundred scholars and artists, to make a study of the country. For three years they gathered mountains of information, made drawings, took notes, and collected art objects, even after Napoleon himself had left. When the British finally won the war, the French scientists went home, taking most of their material with them.

But the most important thing they found did not go home with the French. The British took it and it is now in the British Museum, where you can go and see it, and even touch its smooth surface. It is a piece of black basalt which some French soldiers found at Rosetta, a town near the mouth of the Nile. The Rosetta Stone, as it is called, has three inscriptions carved on its surface. One is in Greek, one is in the ancient hieroglyphics, and the third is in a simplified form of picture-writing called demotic, meaning it was used by ordinary people.

Casts of the stone were sent to scholars to try to decipher, since it was assumed that the text was the same in all three languages. The Greek could be read. It was a letter written in 196 B.C. by the priests of the city of Memphis to their king to thank him for all he had done for them.

After years of study, a Frenchman named Jean François Champollion decoded the hieroglyphics. He was able to do so because he knew Coptic, a version of ancient Egyptian that had been spoken by the early Christians in Egypt.

After that, other inscriptions could be read, and gradually the history of Egypt became clear. It seemed that very long ago Egypt was made up of two separate kingdoms. About 3100 B.C., Menes, the king of Upper Egypt (that is, the southern part, where the Nile rises), conquered Lower Egypt and united the two countries. From that time on, Egypt was ruled by a succession of dynasties. A dynasty was a family of kings, and there were twenty-six dynasties during a period of more than 2,500 years.

The Egyptians believed that after death the spirit lived on as long as the body was intact. So they took care to preserve the bodies of their dead and to bury them with everything they could possibly need in the life to come. The richer and greater the person, the more magnificent was his tomb. That explained the pyramids. They were the tombs of kings. And there were thousands of other tombs, in which lay mummies, the bodies of the dead, preserved by embalming, together with food, furniture, jewelry of gold and precious stones, sculpture, chariots, even ships to carry the dead on their voyage through the sky.

In later graves there were wall paintings, showing how all these things were made. There were scenes of farm life, pictures of jewelers, smiths and carpenters at work. These pictures had a purpose. By their magic, the priests could make all these things real. Therefore, after a time, it was thought not to be necessary to put real food and jewels and clothing into the tomb. Pictures were enough.

And in the dry desert air, the wood and cloth and paint were preserved as fresh as the day they were made. They showed what life had been like in Egypt. The history of the dynasties could be read like a book.

Soon there was a great craze for Egyptian antiquities. People rushed to collect them, not caring what they wrecked. Egyptians as well as foreigners began to strip the tombs to get beautiful things to sell. Much valuable material was lost or thrown away, and many things were taken out of their context with no record of where they had come from.

There were some archaeologists who tried to stop the vandalism, at least to make sure that the greatest treasures of Egypt were not taken out of the country where they belonged. Auguste Édouard Mariette, a French consul, was the first to try to save some of the most beautiful and interesting things for Egypt. Another consul, Maspero, carried on his work.

Then in 1880 there came to Egypt a young man named William Matthew Flinders Petrie, who was to revolutionize archaeology. Petrie wasn't trained as an archaeologist. He had done surveying in his early youth, traveling about England and measuring ancient barrows and stone circles. He came to Egypt to do some surveying in the Great Pyramid because his father's friend, the Royal Astronomer of Scotland, had written a book in which he stated that the measurements of the Pyramid had some mystical astronomical meaning. He proved the book was wrong, and wrote a book of his own about the pyramids. By this time he was so fascinated with Egypt that he stayed there. He worked there until 1926.

Petrie's methods were something new. He invented them as he went along. He was furious with bunglers who blew up tombs with dynamite, shoveled away anything they didn't want, and kept no records. To Petrie everything was important, not just the treasure but the smallest and most insignificant bead or pin, or bit of broken pottery, provided you kept careful records of its find spot and its relation to other things. Nobody thought broken pottery was important, but Petrie made his greatest discoveries by means of it.

Pottery is invaluable to the archaeologist for several reasons. It is made out of clay and therefore is easily broken. The pieces have no value so the owners throw it away, and treasure-seekers don't bother to pick it up. But though pots are breakable, potsherds are indestructible. They never change. They can be fitted together to show the shape and design of the pot. And since pots have always been made according to characteristic styles, they make perfect clues. We can tell from the shape and design where they came from and when they were made.

Petrie used pottery to help fill the gaps in Egyptian history. He invented a technique called cross-dating. If two pieces of pottery (or jewelry or anything else for that matter) were found together, and the date of one was known, the other could be assumed to belong to the same period. The idea was simple, but clever. (Remember that at that time there was still no way of pinning dates on anything.)

At a place called Gurob, Petrie found pottery that seemed to be foreign in style, together with Egyptian objects from the eighteenth dynasty. Later, in Greece, he saw the same kind of pottery he had found at Gurob. He knew then the date of the pottery and could prove that there had been trade between the two countries at that time.

At Kahur in northern Egypt, he found pottery that he thought was from the Aegean islands, together with things from the 12th dynasty. Later, when the Minoan culture in Crete was discovered, this type of pottery was found, and could be dated by the Egyptian evidence.

But Petrie's most important achievement was in an area

Grave of prehistoric Egyptian.

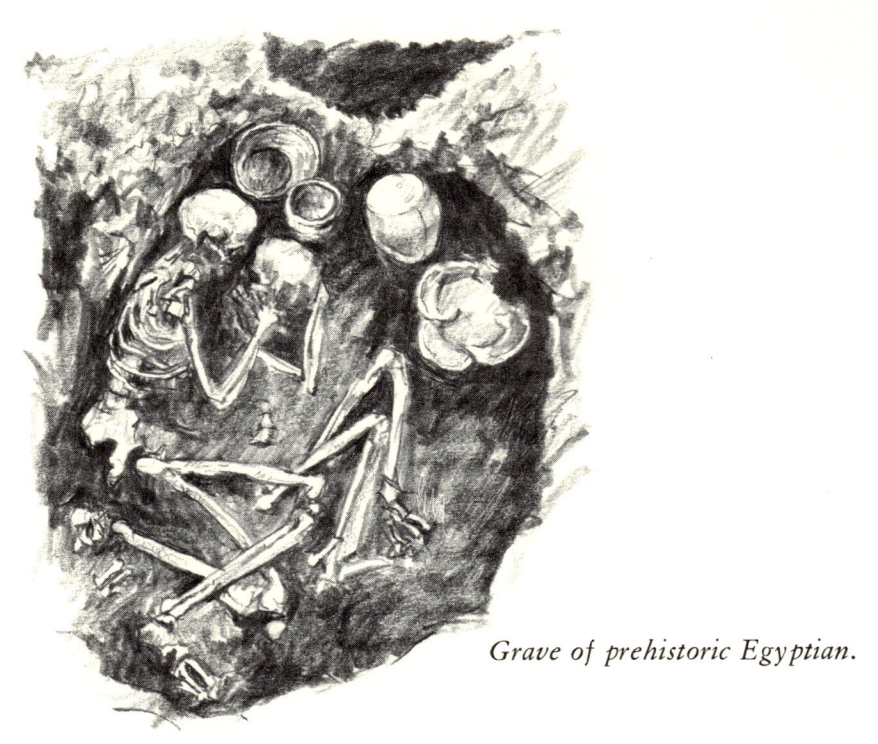

where there were no dates at all.

In 1904, while digging near Nakada in Middle Egypt, he found a cemetery. It was a huge one, with about 2,000 graves. But these were not elegant stone tombs. They were just holes in the ground, and the people buried there were unknown. The grave-goods buried with them were simple. There were flint tools and arrowheads, long blades and polished flint axes. There were a few copper pins but no metal tools. Food had been left in the graves—some bones and grains still remained —in beautiful stone jars of alabaster and basalt, and also in pottery. Some of the pottery was black-topped, some was red with cross-lined designs made to look like basketry, or with pictures of animals, men and boats painted in white. Some of the pots had wavy handles.

Near the cemetery, there were the traces of a large settlement. In the earth were the foundations of huts made of reeds and mud.

Who were these people? There were no hieroglyphics in these graves. There was nothing to show what dynasty they belonged to. In fact they had lived before the earliest dynasty. They were Neolithic farmers.

This was the first unmistakable sign of the beginnings of Egyptian culture. Were there more of these people? Farther north, near Gerzeh, Petrie found another cemetery with many grave-goods, and another settlement. But these people were more advanced. They didn't live in mud huts, but in real houses. There were even traces of doors with wooden frames. They too had some black-topped pottery, but less of it than at Nakada. They had more decorated ware, with red paint on a tan background. They had fine stone vessels, and they had learned to use copper for axes, daggers and knives. Pictures on the pottery showed that they had boats big enough to transport stone.

Again, there were no records to tell who the Gerzeans were or how long ago they had lived. But Petrie invented a way to show which settlements were older and which more recent.

He saw that in all the graves, dynastic and predynastic, there was pottery, and that there were styles in pottery—styles of shape or decoration or method. The styles changed slowly from time to time. Petrie made a chart for each pot. On the chart he indicated the changes in style as he noticed them. To each change he assigned a number, which he called a sequence date. By examining hundreds of pots he was able to say which ones of a certain type were older and which more recent. The sequence date began with thirty and ran to eighty, thus leaving space for new discoveries. Whenever a pot was found it was given a number, and though Petrie didn't know exactly how old it was, at least he could tell where it belonged in the sequence. There were nearly always several types of pots in each grave, as well as other objects, and thus these other objects could be sequence-dated along with the pot whose number was known.

Very soon the value of sequence dating was proven. Petrie's students and co-workers, going on where he left off, found still earlier settlements.

Near Badari, on a low spur of desert between the high cliffs and the cultivated fields, new cemeteries were found. The people in these graves had been farmers too, but their culture was simpler. They had no metal. They lived in houses made of wattle or reed, covered with mud or skins or matting. (At least this is the theory, because although no traces of houses have been found, some of the graves contained what looked like models of such houses.) They had barley and wheat, which they reaped with stone-toothed sickles and stored in clay silos. Bread and porridge were found in some of the graves, and the bones of domestic animals, oxen, sheep and goats. They hunted game and birds and caught fish. They had flint tools —saw-edged knives, polished hand-axes and arrowheads, but no long blades. Their pottery was black-topped like the Gerzean, or brown with a rippled design.

The Gerzeans had worn almost no clothes, but the Badarians must have lived through a colder time, for they wore skins with the fur inside, as well as woven lined clothes. Many of the people were buried in linen and skins. And they loved ornaments. There were bracelets, necklaces and anklets. The men liked to wear one large bead on neck or arm. The women and children wore necklaces of beads and shells, and the young girls wore girdles and headbands of shells. The women wore combs in their long braided hair.

Not far from Badari was Der Tasa, where a similar people had lived, but their culture was still simpler. They had rough flints and grain-grinders. Many blackened cooking pots were found. Some of the pottery was like the Badarian, with rippled surfaces as if made with a comb, and some was black-topped like the Gerzean. Again, there were no houses, but grain was stored in holes in the ground.

The bodies in the graves lay mostly on their left sides facing west, often with their hands before their faces, and frequently a body was buried in a kind of hamper of sticks and reeds, a sort of woven coffin. A child's grave had a pillow filled with chaff for the small head to rest on. At the child's feet was a little rough bowl, in front of its face two pots and some calf ribs.

Petrie's foresight in starting his sequence dates with the number 30 could be seen. The Badarian and Tasian pottery fitted in before 30.

Going northward, archaeologists found a village near Merimde, a primitive place with oval-shaped mud huts on the southwest edge of the Delta. Each hut had been about nine by fourteen feet, with a clay pot in the middle of the floor, perhaps to drain off water. There was a communal granary, consisting of pits in the ground lined with basketwork. These people were farmers too. They raised barley and wheat, vetch, or wild peas, and flax which they wove into linen. They had cattle and pigs, but depended heavily on hunting and fishing.

Then, going back even farther in time, two of Petrie's followers found a still earlier settlement. West of the Nile is a great oasis called the Fayum. Ages ago, there was a vast lake here. On the site of the old lake shore, traces of hunter-fishers can be found. Perhaps they came from the North African prairie, for in those days North Africa was not a desert. We know now that this was 5,000 years B.C., and a time of heavy rainfall. What is now the Sahara Desert was park and meadow land. In the lake lived crocodiles, hippopotamuses and fish. The people who camped there used bone harpoons and left their stone arrowheads and axes in the rubbish heaps beside the lake.

A little later, farmers lived there. They planted and harvested grain, using reaping knives made of tiny flint blades set in grooved wooden handles.

The Fayumis stored their grain in silos which were holes in the earth lined with basketry. They ground it in stone mortars or querns. They kept sheep, or perhaps goats, and cattle and pigs. They wove linen, had plain, rough pottery, and cut trees with polished stone axes.

They were the earliest farmers in Africa, but there is no sign that their farming began there. They were farmers when they arrived. Before them were only the hunter-fishers, and earlier still, only a few flint axes in the terraces above the Nile showed where some Palaeolithic hunters had wandered, many thousands of years ago.

As the archaeologists in Switzerland had to admit, the idea of agriculture was not from here. Where then had it come from?

There were clues. Other things had come to Egypt by the overland route from Palestine, and across the Red Sea.

The use of copper, lead and silver began in Asia, where the Egyptians went for their raw materials.

Reaping knife with flint teeth, from the Fayum.

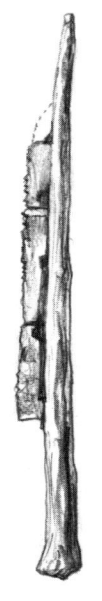

Styles of house-building in the earliest dynasties were like those of Southwest Asia. There, houses were built of mud-brick, hardened in the sun. The first Egyptian houses were built this way. It was natural for Mesopotamia, where there was almost no stone. But in Egypt, there was plenty of building stone, and later buildings were made of it. Obviously the original idea had come from the East.

Petrie himself, working in Palestine, had found the same sort of wavy-handled pottery as that in the graves at Nakada.

Even the fishhooks and harpoons and the flint-edged sickles found in the Fayum were made like the ones dug up from the floors of Palestinian caves.

But the most convincing clue was this: sheep and goats, wheat and barley, were not native to Egypt, but to another land, farther east. The beginnings of Egypt's culture were lost in the mists of time. But eastward was a culture older still.

4 ❧ The Near East

Eastward of Egypt lies the Red Sea, and the Sinai Peninsula where the Egyptians used to go to get copper and turquoise. East of that is the part of Asia that is called the Near East, or the Middle East. It is a vast plain surrounded by mountains, and it has been carved into several countries. Bordering the Mediterranean is Jordan. North of that is Israel, and south of it is Saudi Arabia. Most of this area was once called Palestine.

North of Israel is Syria, and beyond that is Turkey, which the Greeks called Anatolia. This is the Greek name for sunrise, and, of course, to the Greeks that land was the East, where the sun rose.

Traveling eastward, you come to two great rivers, the Euphrates and the Tigris, flowing southeast through the plain. The land between the rivers was once called Mesopotamia (that is what the name means); now it is Iraq. Still farther east is Iran, or Persia.

All during the Middle Ages, the Near East was almost unknown to Europeans. Much of it is a desert. Only along the rivers and in the mountains is it green. Most of the people who live there are Mohammedans, and for centuries Mohammedans and Christians were bitter enemies.

So only a few Europeans ever ventured into this land of danger and mystery. Some of those who did go were merchants, some were simply curious about strange places, and some were seeking the places mentioned in the Bible.

For all that was known about the early history of the human race then came from the Bible, and it all seemed to have begun in this part of the world. Somewhere out here the Garden of Eden was supposed to have been, and Mount Ararat where Noah's Ark landed after the Flood. Somewhere on the banks of the Euphrates, Noah's sons had settled down and become shepherds. And somewhere here was the "plain in the land of Shinar." Here Noah's descendants tried to build a tower called Babel, which was to reach to Heaven itself. It was from Ur, in this region, that Abraham went westward to Canaan (another name for Palestine) to settle with his tribe and his flocks. And it was from Nineveh that the Assyrian kings, Shalmaneser, Sargon, Sennacherib and Nebuchadnezzar, went forth to conquer the world, and brought the Jews back to captivity in Babylon.

All these names and these stories were very familiar. Were they true? Did these things happen or were they merely legends? It might be reassuring to know.

So travelers set out to find Babylon, and Ur of the Chaldees,

A tell: Tepe Siyalk, Iran.

and mighty Nineveh. But they did not find these places.

In the swamps along the rivers they found the Marsh Arabs living in a strange world of reeds and water, herding water buffaloes from boats, fishing, snaring water birds, and building houses of reeds and mud. They had been living this way for centuries, and they still do.

Elsewhere, outside of cities like Baghdad, Mosul, and Aleppo, they found only native villages built of dusty mud bricks, desert sands, and here and there huge tells—the Arab name for mounds—like flat-topped hills rising from the plains. Who had built these mysterious mounds? Nobody knew. There were stories that one large group of them, on the Tigris across from the modern city of Mosul, was Nineveh, and that another heap on the Euphrates, near Baghdad, was ancient Babylon.

There were no records. But here and there, among the mounds and the sands, curious, square tablets of clay had been found, covered with queer marks. Was this some strange form of decoration? Nobody knew. But now and then travelers collected these funny things and sent them to museums, and there they lay, gathering dust.

Then, in the middle of the nineteenth century, just as in Egypt, an interest in Near Eastern antiquities developed. The French consul, at Mosul, Paul Émile Botta, had been sent there in 1840 because he had had experience in Egypt and knew a little about excavating.

To Kuyunjik, near Mosul on the Tigris, Botta went with some workmen, and began to dig in one of the mounds there. He was really lucky. Very soon he found walls of mud-brick, and fantastically carved stone figures of men and animals. It was the magnificent palace of an Assyrian king. He immediately hired more workmen and had them dig out everything they could find. Just as in Egypt, his main purpose was to send home as much as possible for the museums. The workmen hacked away at the mound, destroying many priceless treasures that had lain safely in the earth for thousands of years. The very thought of it is enough to make modern archaeologists gnash their teeth. Nobody cared about guarding these treasures.

Some of the statues were stolen and burned by the peasants to make gypsum for plastering their houses. Some were broken. The rest were hauled to the Tigris and floated downriver on rafts to the Persian Gulf, where they were loaded on ships. Some of the rafts were lost by accident en route, and others were deliberately sunk by Arabs.

In 1842 Austen Henry Layard came to Mesopotamia. He was a brilliant young Englishman who was fascinated by the Mesopotamian ruins, but had no money to do any excavating. He knew a great deal about the East, however, and was of great service to the English ambassador at Constantinople. This gentleman, who was also interested in archaeology, finally supplied Layard with funds so that he could start digging.

Layard became the most famous of Assyriologists. He sent

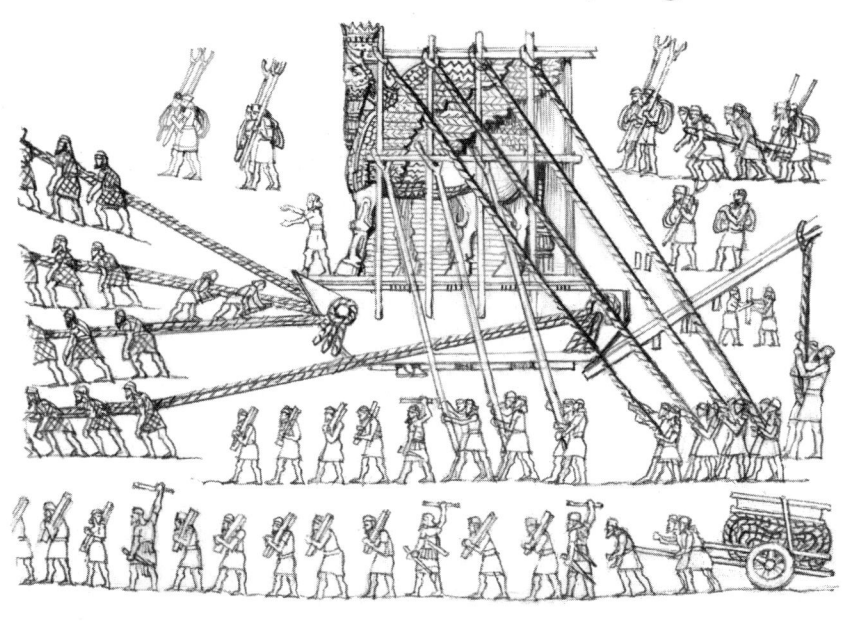

Drawing of bas relief, wall decoration from Kuyunjik, showing winged bull being moved by Assyrians.

home huge shipments of carved slabs, great stone winged bulls, and tablets inscribed with those markings which nobody could read. His descriptions of the method of moving these things make one shudder. The huge bulls, weighing twenty tons or more, had to be moved on wooden carts with teams of oxen, and lifted with pulleys and ropes. The onlookers expected the whole thing to crash at any moment. As a result of Layard's efforts the British Museum now has the world's best collection of Assyrian art.

But the most important thing he found was not winged bulls or sculptures of kings.

In 1849, Layard excavated the mounds opposite Mosul where Nineveh had been thought to be. He did find Nineveh. He found the royal palace of King Sennacherib, who had ruled from 704 to 681 B.C. And in a room in the palace, a foot deep from wall to wall, he found an enormous collection of clay tablets, inscribed with those curious markings called cuneiform, which means wedge-shaped.

By now people knew what those markings were. They were writing. And these tablets were the king's library. A little later another great library was found, this one belonging to King Ashur-bani-pal, Sennacherib's grandson.

And at last, thanks to another Englishman, the cuneiform script was finally deciphered. Henry Creswicke Rawlinson, who had been a British counsul at Baghdad, had been working on this problem for years.

Imagine what a problem it was. There were masses of tablets, sculptures, walls, rocks, all covered with markings like hens' tracks, with no relation to any known script.

Just as the Egyptologists found a clue in the Rosetta Stone, Rawlinson found one on an enormous cliff called the Rock of Darius, a sheer wall of rock in Persia, at a place called Behistun. Here was an inscription which seemed to be in three languages, only they were all written in the same cuneiform script. The Rosetta Stone was easy by comparison. There at least one language was readable.

However, Rawlinson had great imagination and determination, and he did at last decipher the script. Then the tablets could be read, and gradually the whole history of Assyria became known. But there was much more than history. Ashur-bani-pal's library contained all the knowledge of his time: mathematics, medicine, religion, legend. It seemed that he had been a highly intelligent man, and had ordered schol-

Clay tablet with cuneiform writing.

ars to collect all this material so that it should not be forgotten.

It took years for modern scholars to put it all in order and transcribe it, for of course the tablets were rather mixed up. As the scholars worked, they found new mysteries. It seemed that much of the material was copied from older records. There were dictionaries explaining words no longer in use, like our Latin and Greek dictionaries. There were references to ancient persons, such as "the Kings of Sumer and Akkad." What was Sumer? What was Akkad?

Among the tablets were some that told the story of a great flood, and of a king or folk-hero named Gilgamesh who built a ship to escape from it. The ship floated for seven days, and finally came to rest on a mountain. Then a dove was sent forth to find dry land.

It sounded very much like the Bible story of Noah. Could the Assyrians have had a flood story too? No, this did not sound like an Assyrian story. Assyria was high and rocky and dry, and this was a story of a very different land, low and flat, where floods might be quite common. Such a land was southern Mesopotamia, a plain which was mostly desert in dry times, but might be very wet when its two rivers were in flood.

Around 1850, William Loftus, a geologist, traveled in southern Mesopotamia. He found a desert criss-crossed by the remains of canals, once an irrigation system. He found mounds or tells of mud-brick, the ruins of ancient cities. He

A ziggurat in Iran, after excavation; originally 165 feet high, 345 feet long.

found ziggurats, towers of solid mud-brick. He dug in the ruins known as Warka, his feet buried in sand at every step, and he found clay tablets there which he sent to Rawlinson. On one of them Rawlinson read the name "Erech." Now Erech was another name for "Uruk," the city ruled by Gilgamesh, in the flood story from Nineveh. And this name was also mentioned in Genesis, which says: "And Cush begat Nimrod. . . . He was a mighty hunter before the Lord. . . . And the beginning of his kingdom was Babel, and Erech, and Accad, and Calneh, in the land of Shinar."

It appeared that Warka was the modern name for Erech or Uruk. The ancient stories were true. There had been a civilization here, older and earlier than that of the Assyrians or the Babylonians, so long ago that its very existence had been forgotten. It was Sumer. Its Biblical name was Shinar.

Little by little, the history of the Sumerians emerged. They had drained the marshes and built cities: Eridu, perhaps the oldest city on earth; Ur, the birthplace of Abraham; Erech and Kish, Nippur and Lagash. Ur and Eridu had once been busy seaports. Where now there was desert, 4,000 years ago the river waters had flowed beside their walls.

The Sumerians invented writing, the plow and the wheel. They had a code of law, science and mathematics, as well as fine art and literature.

Each city had its temple in the form of a ziggurat or step-tower of solid mud-brick, on top of which dwelt the god of the place. The god of Eridu was En-ki, of whom it was said, "When En-ki rose, the fishes rose and adored him."

The high priest of each temple was the king or ruler of the city, who enforced the laws, made war and levied taxes.

There were great farms, orchards and vineyards, irrigated by canals that brought water from the rivers, for the Sumerians were skilled engineers. It was these farms, worked by thousands of peasants, that produced the food supply which made everything else possible: armies of soldiers, artisans, artists, priests. Surplus grain was the basis of trade needed to get stone for monuments, gold and precious stones for jewelry, iron and copper for tools and weapons.

The Sumerians, called the Black-Headed People, were conquered about 2360 B.C. by the Akkadians north of them. After that their kings were called "the Kings of Sumer and Akkad." About 1792 B.C. the Babylonians conquered the whole country, and in the thirteenth century B.C., the Assyrians overran it, and in time Sumer was forgotten.

But where had the Sumerians come from? Clues were needed, and as archaeology became a science for professionals, instead of a hobby for amateurs, they were found. The clues were pottery.

In 1926, Sir Leonard Woolley, working for the British Museum and the University of Pennsylvania, was getting ready to excavate the huge mounds at Ur. (The Arabs used the place as a source of bricks. They called it Tel Muqayyer, meaning Mound of Pitch, because of the pitch or petroleum which the ancient builders had used for mortar.) But before undertaking this very important dig, Woolley decided to start somewhere else first. In this way his workmen would get practice and be more skillful when they came to the bigger job. At a small tell called Al 'Ubaid, a few miles away, a little Sumerian temple had been found, so Woolley went there.

In the middle of a wide stretch of desert sand, digging deep down, he found the remains of a village. It was not very impressive. There were bits of reed matting, stuck together with clay mixed with pitch or dung. These were the remains of houses, and among them were pieces of pottery, some dark green with geometrical designs painted in black, some with a tan background. Digging beneath this level, Woolley found clean soil, laid down by the river.

To Woolley this meant that thousands of years ago, this had been a little island in the middle of the river, on which people had built their reed huts, just as today the Marsh Arabs build their houses of the same kind of reeds. The pottery was named 'Ubaid ware.

Woolley went back to Ur. He worked there for several years and found the remains of a magnificent culture. Ur had been a port on the Euphrates River, a city with large houses of plastered brick. Its artisans had made beautiful mosaics, jewelry, musical instruments and sculpture.

Woolley decided to find out whether this high culture had not developed from something simpler. He had his workmen dig down, straight through layers of mud-bricks, ashes, pottery sherds and other debris. They dug a huge pit, sixty-four feet deep. And at the bottom, beneath everything, were pieces of 'Ubaid ware.

The people who left them there were the first inhabitants

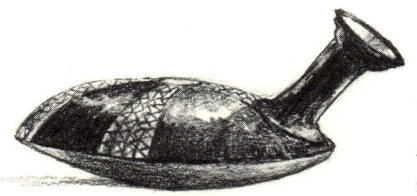

Pottery jar: 'Ubaid ware; reconstructed.

of southern Mesopotamia. They were farmers. They planted grain, hoed it with flint-headed hoes, and cut it with sickles set with flint teeth. They had sheep and goats. They made little clay figures of animals and women, to use in their religious rites, as all early people seem to have done to encourage fertility.

Where did the 'Ubaidians come from? Far to the east, in the highlands of Iran, similar greenish or tan pottery and similar figurines have been found. Persia was their original home, and they were farmers when they came to Sumer. The 'Ubaidians brought with them their skills, their animals and seeds. Probably they were looking for new land. The head of the Persian Gulf was much farther north then than it is now. As the rivers brought silt down from the north and new land rose out of the swamps, they took possession of it.

The 'Ubaidians built their curved huts of reeds, their temples on platforms of mud. They made boats for fishing. They hunted animals and water birds, and planted their crops. They were the first people to live in southern Iraq. As the Sumerian legend said, "All the lands were sea, then Eridu was made."

The first villages, dating back to 4325 B.C., were primitive. But the population grew. The land away from the rivers, though dry, was very fertile, and they learned to irrigate it. This was a challenge. It developed their skill, and their ability to work together. Soon the land was producing large amounts of food. They built large towns of sun-dried brick. Their temples became ziggurats, huge piles of mud-brick towering above the cities. They founded the civilization called Sumerian.

As the population grew and the cities became crowded, they began to move northward.

But though they were the first people in southern Iraq, they were not the first in the north. There was an earlier culture.

In 1929, German archaeologists were digging near the headwaters of the Euphrates River in a mound called Tell Halaf. They found a new and very handsome kind of painted pottery. Some pieces were covered with pictures of people and animals, others with geometrical patterns of lines, circles

Halafian pottery with geometrical design.

and dots in red and black. The pottery was so much better than 'Ubaid ware that it seemed as if the Halafians must have been later arrivals, but this was not so. They were always found at a lower level.

For a long while nothing more was known about them. But in recent years a great many Halafian sites have been found, all the way to the Mediterranean Sea. The people lived in villages of two-roomed houses, each with a domed roof and a long entrance room. They had bake-ovens and storage pits. The Halafians were farmers. Hundreds of flint sickle blades were found, shiny from cutting grain, as well as the grain itself, wheat and barley. There was also flax, grown perhaps for linen, but more likely for the oil in the seeds.

There were many figurines of women, as well as of goats, sheep, dogs and cattle. There were arrowheads and sling-stones, and clay models of wild animals, showing that the people were hunters as well as farmers. And they were great traders, for there was obsidian from Lake Van and shells from as far away as the Indian Ocean. Obviously they were a vigorous and artistic people.

But the later Halafian remains are sparse and poor. There are signs of disturbance and poverty. And then come the pieces of 'Ubaid ware, a few at first, and then more and more. What happened?

The story seems clear. The settlers from the south had moved northward. As their population exploded, they needed room to expand. They overran their northern neighbors and wiped them out.

Until 1931, Halaf culture was the earliest known. In that year some English archaeologists, working near Nineveh, dug a deep pit below the foundations of an Assyrian temple. They planned to dig down to virgin soil. Down, down, they went, building a spiral staircase along the sides of the shaft, which got narrower as they descended. As they dug, they found samples of all the stages of the history of Iraq—pottery, beads, figurines—until at last they reached the brightly painted Halaf ware, seventy feet down in the earth. And beneath them, on virgin soil, were eleven potsherds scratched with a strange design. At the time, there was no other evidence of the earliest settlers of northern Iraq. And for some years there would be none.

5 ❧ *New Ways in Archaeology*

A world war had been brewing, like an unwanted but inevitable storm. In 1939, it began. Work came to a halt. The archaeologists who had been working side by side, Americans, Germans and English, packed up their belongings, closed their camps, and left for home. Not until the war was over would they return. However, when they did, it was with new energy, and also with new techniques.

Of course even before the war digging methods were far different from those of the old days. In those times, even Austen Henry Layard would hire a gang of native workers, order them to hack a trench through a tell, pick out what looked good, and shovel the rest back into the hole.

Layard's assistant, Hormuzd Rassam, actually had several gangs scattered about the countryside, and visited them from time to time to see what they had found. Between visits they were on their own!

Archaeology in those days was pick-and-shovel work, or, sometimes, a delightful picnic, even back home in England.

A story in a magazine of 1852 tells of some ladies and gentlemen who spent the day watching some laborers dig a barrow on a hill in Kent. They brought along plenty of good things to eat, and put in the time eating and drinking and playing games, occasionally giving orders to the laborers. When the rain came pouring down, they had to take shelter with their umbrellas in the barrow itself. It was all great fun!

Now, however, archaeologists worked as if they were handling jewels. Workmen were carefully trained, and were never allowed to work without an expert in charge.

Test trenches were dug, to be sure the site was the right one. The ground was divided into grids, the earth scraped away from each square, bones and pottery dusted off with camel-hair brushes, washed and numbered, and records kept of every sherd and bead that turned up.

Archaeologists now worked in teams. A geologist would be needed to study the soil layers, the rocks, the effect of glaciation and anything else the earth might contain.

A botanist went along to study plant material, living or dead. He might find information in unexpected places. For instance, with the microscope he might examine the soil from a village site and find bits of gray material that looked like ash. The cell structure of this stuff shows that it comes from reeds. There are no traces of houses in the area, so perhaps the people built huts of the kind of reeds that grow there even now.

Layout for excavation in form of grid. Each square is numbered; found objects are marked correspondingly.

The palaeobotanist knows that pottery is often tempered with straw or leaves to make the clay stick together. Sometimes the potters used wheat or barley straw, picked up from the ground where it was threshed. If there is some of this in the pottery, the botanist may be able to tell whether the wheat was wild or cultivated.

A zoologist went with the team to examine animals' bones, to try to learn what animals they came from, whether wild or tame, and perhaps he might deduce what the climate was like when they were alive.

But the most spectacular of the new developments was a way of giving specific dates to found objects. This had always been guesswork. A hundred years ago, geologists would guess at the age of a deposit by estimating how long it had taken for the strata to be laid down. This method sometimes resulted in some wild guesses.

A Swedish geologist named DeGeer had found a way of dating events back to 10,000 B.C. in lands where there had been glaciers. He did this by counting the deposits, or varves, left by the melting ice at the edge of the glacier each year. Of course this method was of no use in Mesopotamia.

Another Swede, Lennart von Post, had found pollen grains preserved in the peat beds of ancient lakes. From the pollen at different levels he could tell what sort of trees had grown there. He could show the northern limits of forests at different times, and give a pretty accurate date to anything found in peat back to the Ice Age.

Petrie's method of sequence-dating, of course, could only be relative, unless one date was positively known.

But in the 1940's a method was found that would give specific dates to objects from unknown periods. It came from atomic chemistry and was one of the more useful results of the work on the atom bomb.

It was found that some elements have radioactive forms called isotopes. One of the elements is carbon, which is part of every living thing, plant or animal.

Now living things are constantly absorbing carbon. Plants get it from the carbon dioxide in the air, and animals get it from the plants they eat. They are also constantly giving it out, so the amount of carbon in their bodies remains constant as long as they are alive. When they die, they stop taking in carbon. Usually their bodies decay and disappear. But in some cases they are preserved in one way or another.

Now it happens that an isotope of carbon, called Carbon 14, 14 being its atomic weight, exists in tiny amounts in the atmosphere. It comes from Carbon 12 (ordinary carbon) that has been bombarded by cosmic rays from outer space. All living things contain a constant tiny amount of C-14 along with the ordinary C-12.

Carbon 14, being radioactive, is unstable, and constantly breaks down, but as long as life goes on it is always renewed. Thus all living things are slightly radioactive to the same degree.

But as soon as a plant or animal dies, it stops taking in C-14, and what is there continues to break down, eventually becoming nitrogen. And it breaks down at a fixed rate. In 5,568 years, half of it is gone. In another 5,568 years, half of the remainder is gone, and so on. Therefore its half-life is said to be 5,568.

Dr. Willard C. Libby of the University of Chicago devised a way of using this half-life to measure the amount of C-14 in organic material, compared to the amount of C-12. This would give the age of things that had been preserved in the earth for centuries. To put it simply, if some charcoal from an ancient hearth gives half as many clicks on the Geiger counter as some new charcoal, the old charcoal must be 5,568 years old. If it gives half as many again, it should be 11,136 years old.

Of course the test is not as accurate as that. Often the amounts of test material are too small, or are contaminated with dirt and dust from the air, or from things around them. So the date may be given as 5,000 plus or minus 275 years. Then too, as we go back in time, the amount of C-14 becomes too small to measure, so the test does not work farther back than 70,000 years.

But with all its imperfections it is still a marvelous tool. When the archaeologists came back to work, it proved its worth at once.

Work had not come to a complete standstill during the war. Strange to say, no bombs fell on Iraq. The Antiquities Department there had some young men who went right on digging without the help of foreigners.

In 1943, they were working at Hassuna, twenty miles south of Nineveh. There, on a small mound, they found some potsherds like the ones found in 1931 at Nineveh, below the Halaf level, at the very bottom of the great shaft. They had the same scratched designs. But here they were on the surface.

Also among the grass blades were flint tools, bone needles, little pottery figures, and near the surface, the foundations of mud-walled houses.

It was the earliest real village found so far, and it was possible to give it a date—a real date, not just a comparative one. Carbon 14 tests placed it between 5100 and 5600 B.C., ± 250 years.

Soon other sites like Hassuna were found, with the same kind of pottery, though the later ones showed a painted kind known as Samarran. The outlines in the earth showed small houses built of puddled mud very much as Arab houses are built today. (A course of soft mud about six inches high is patted into place and allowed to dry in the sun. Then another course is laid, and so on.)

The houses had several little rooms with reed mats on the floors. They had ovens, and storage pits lined with pitch. The people were farmers. They kept sheep and goats, and sometimes pigs. They raised grain, and ground it in querns or hand mills. They depended on farming—this was plain.

And all these villages were located in a great crescent-shaped arc that extended from the Persian Gulf, north through Iraq, west to the Mediterranean coast and south into Egypt. This was the area called the Fertile Crescent. In 1916, a famous scholar, Professor James Breasted, invented that name for it. This great horseshoe was the borderland between the mountains on the north and the desert on the south. And it was this fertile fringe, Breasted thought, that was the most important early home of men in western Asia.

But the evidence showed that though the Fertile Crescent was an early home of men, it was not the first. The archaeologists were getting very warm, but they had not yet found what they were looking for.

6 ❧ Jarmo

In 1948, Dr. Robert Braidwood of the University of Chicago and his wife, Linda, were excavating at Matarrah, a village site in the foothills of the Kurdish Mountains. This is the Zagros Range between Iraq and Iran. At Matarrah there was pottery of the Hassuna type. This was another of those early villages, interesting in itself, but the Braidwoods were even more interested when someone told them of a site about sixty miles away, where there was a mound that had never been dug.

The mound was called Jarmo, and it was on the edge of a wadi, a dried-up stream bed, way off the beaten track, near some Arab villages of mud-walled houses. When Dr. Braidwood got there, he saw at once that it was a settlement site. Bits of worked flint and obsidian were lying on the ground. The mound itself had never been disturbed, except where the rain had washed away one side. The eroded side showed about twenty-five feet of occupation levels. Bits of pottery could be seen in the upper levels, and below, flints were stick-

Jarmo, seen from across wadi. Expedition buildings and photographic tower at the top.

ing out and there were dark streaks that probably meant hearths, or cooking fires.

Dr. Braidwood knew he was on the verge of an important discovery. He went home to prepare for an expedition.

This was very different from the earlier type of expedition. Now one had to obtain grants of money from foundations or universities and also recruit a qualified staff: a geologist, a palaeozoologist, a palaeobotanist, and some graduate students who wanted experience and would work even without pay.

Mountains of supplies had to be bought, living quarters arranged and permission to excavate obtained. Then an arrangement had to be made for sharing anything that was found. In the past, the excavators used to ship home the best things they found, but now the host country has first choice, which is as it should be.

At last the expedition started. They set up camp near the mound and hired a staff of Arabs to do the digging. The men had to be carefully trained to work gently with their small picks, clearing away the soil a little at a time so as not to destroy walls or living floors, and carrying their finds in labeled baskets back to camp to be sorted, washed and studied. It was hard, dusty work.

But it was not long before Braidwood saw that in this mound he had something very interesting.

Such a mound, or tell, grows from hundreds of years of human living. Long ago, people came and built houses or huts of sun-dried mud, like adobe, sometimes with stone foundations. They made roofs of branches and brush covered with plaster made of mud. Such houses are fine as long as it does not rain too much. If they are patched up, they may last twenty or thirty years. But finally they fall to pieces, and the owner builds a new house nearby; a little later someone may build a new house on top of the old one. So the tell grows.

An occupation level may represent about thirty years. As the archaeologist digs down, he finds the stumps of the walls at each level. He also finds the things the houseowner left behind when he moved away. These objects differ from one generation to the next, and this tells us something about the people who lived there. If the pottery or flint tools are a little different, it may mean just a change in style. Or perhaps some foreigners moved in and added their little touches. If the styles are very different, it may mean a new population entirely. Perhaps all people moved away and new ones came, or perhaps the original settlers were wiped out.

At Jarmo, the population seemed to be pretty uniform. There were sixteen levels, and Braidwood figured that that meant the place had been occupied for about 400 years, counting perhaps 25 years for each level.

In most levels there were bowls and cups of stone, beautifully ground, as well as axes, querns and mortars. There were chipped flints, including many microliths, and tools and jewelry of finely carved bone.

The houses were small, but carefully built. The rooms were only about two yards square, but each house had several rooms. It was a small village, with never more than twenty houses or perhaps 150 people at any one time, but it was a permanent village. There were clay-lined basins for hearths, and baskets lined with pitch for storing food. There had even been doors that swung on stone pivots. Nobody builds that way if they don't mean to stay.

How old was Jarmo? Carbon 14 tests were made. For some

reason the results were puzzling. The tests showed at least twelve different dates running from 3250 to 9250 B.C. Braidwood decided that the most reasonable date was 6750 ± 200 B.C. Hassuna, the next in age, went back to a time between 5100 and 5600 B.C.

But there was a curious thing about Jarmo. Except in the top few layers, there was no pottery—only stone. Never before had a permanent village site been found without pottery.

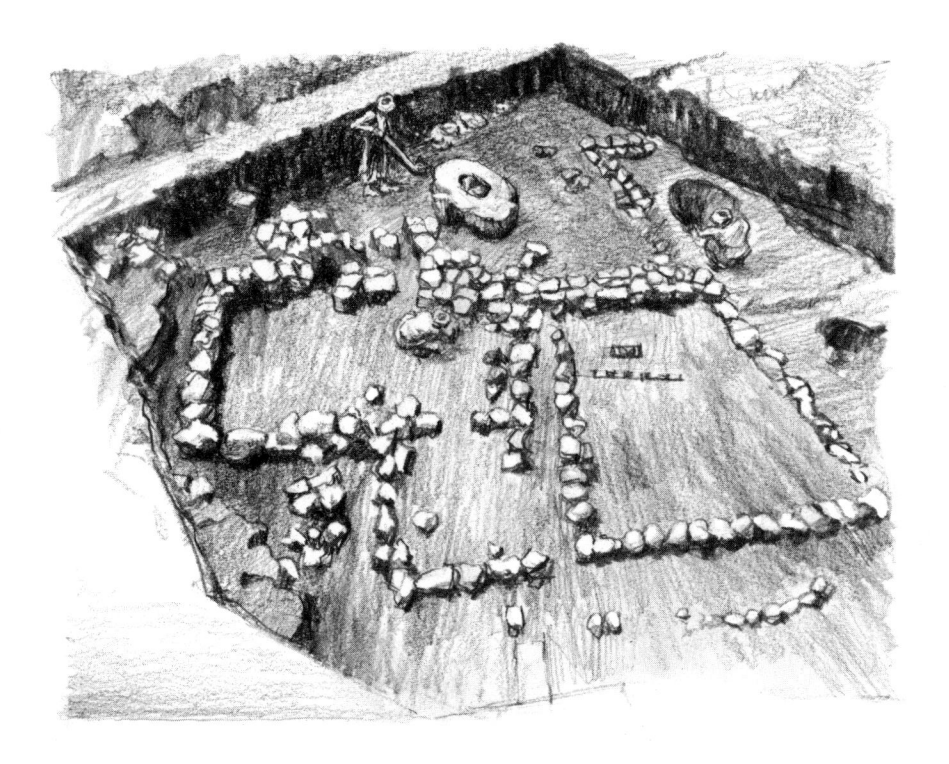

Excavation at Jarmo showing stone house foundations and round clay-lined ovens.

Pottery had long been considered the sign of the settled farming village. And this *was* a farming village.

In the clay-lined hearths were charred grains of wheat and barley. In the floors were impressions of grains dropped there and perhaps pressed into the soft clay by a human foot. These impressions could be used as molds. Soft plaster pressed into them gave perfect models of grains 9,000 years old.

Now these *could* have been wild grains, gathered by the women of the village and then roasted and ground for good. They were like the wild wheat and barley that grow to this day in the foothills of the Zagros mountains where Jarmo lies. But they were not *quite* like them. There was a difference.

The seeds or grains of any wheat grow in a spike at the top of the stalk. The spike of the wild wheat is very brittle when it is ripe. It breaks up into spikelets which scatter over the ground. This is how the wheat seeds itself. But cultivated wheat has tough stalks. The spikelets do not scatter but have to be beaten or threshed before the grain is loosened. This is useful. It means the wheat can be cut and carried home.

Some of the Jarmo wheat and barley were the cultivated

Hand mill shaped like mortar and pestle.

kind, with bits of stalk still hanging to the grains. But not all. Some were still like the wild grains. It seemed clear that the Jarmo people had begun to cultivate grain, but had not been doing it long enough for all the wheat and barley to lose their wild character.

There were bones of goats, sheep, pigs, gazelles and a few cattle. From the shape of the goat horns and the shortness of their leg bones, it seemed that they must be tame. But the sheep and pigs were probably wild, and the cattle almost certainly.

It looked as though these archaeologists had found what they were looking for—a picture of the first farmers. This is how food production started. This is how the people lived— so long ago that they didn't even have pottery yet—in settled villages, close to the place where the wild plants and animals were found, beginning to take some of those plants and animals for their own, to keep them close. Jarmo may not itself be the oldest Neolithic village, but it gives a picture of what such a village was like.

They hunted too—the gazelle bones proved that. And they probably had dogs to help with the hunting. There were no dog bones at Jarmo. But among the foundations were little clay figures of dogs, with their tails curled up over their backs.

They gathered wild nuts and acorns, and ate peas and lentils, wild or cultivated.

Since Jarmo was discovered, many other similar village

sites have been found. And they are not where Breasted predicted they would be, in the Fertile Crescent, but in the foothills of the mountains above the Crescent, on the gentle slopes and valleys where the wheat and barley grew wild and where there was plenty of winter and spring rain. All the way from Iran and into southern Turkey and the Jordan Valley and even on the island of Cyprus in the Mediterranean were the settlements of the earliest village farmers.

They weren't all alike. Tepe Sarab, in Iran, had wheat and domesticated sheep, but its houses were only reed huts, so this may have been merely a camping spot. A village at Hacilar in Turkey had houses with red-stained plaster walls, and barley, wheat and lentils, but no domesticated animals except a dog. Some of them are more like Hassuna, a little more advanced, with better houses and pottery, and closer to the Fertile Crescent itself. Maybe the people were starting to move down the mountains to the plains. It is hard to tell. Remember, they weren't all one people. New groups kept moving in from the east, from the north, and from the west.

One thing is sure. All of them were beginning to be farmers. The second greatest invention had taken hold and started to spread.

7 ⚜ The Natufians

In the mountains of Judea and Carmel, facing the sea, there are caves and rock ledges where people, and even ape-men, coming up from Africa, have found shelter for hundreds of thousands of years. Some of the caves had flat terraces out in front. They made good dwelling places. Down below were marshes and woods where fish and wild animals could be caught.

In the 1930's, Dr. Dorothy Garrod, an English archaeologist, was working in one of these caves called Wadi-en-Natuf. She was looking for the remains of palaeolithic men, and she found some Neanderthal-type skeletons.

She also found something else. While digging down through the many levels of the cave floor, she came upon bones of bear and leopard, and a great many gazelles. With them were stone tools—barbed points, scrapers and borers of flint. Many of these were microliths. The people who had left these things came later than palaeolithic men, but long before the villagers of the Fertile Crescent, long before Jarmo,

Mt. Carmel. Dark hollows mark caves where ancient men lived. Expedition tents in foreground.

which of course had not yet been discovered. They were hunters, and depended on wild animals for their food, and probably on any vegetable food they could gather—nuts, berries, fruits.

But there were signs that they ate something else. Among the tools buried in the cave floor were bone handles in which tiny flints had been set to make a cutting blade. Some of the handles were beautifully carved to represent animal heads. The interesting thing about these tools was that there was a glossy sheen on the flint blades. This could only have come from one thing—from the silica in the stems of grass. These tools were sickles. They had been used for reaping grass. What kind of grass?

On the mountain slopes in Palestine, as in the Zagros Mountains of Iraq, grow two kinds of wild grass with edible seeds. They grew there ten thousand years ago as well. They are wild wheat and barley. The Natufians, as those cave-dwellers are now called, must have reaped it. Did that mean they planted it? This question started endless discussions, since no actual grain was found.

Some people pointed out that the grain couldn't have been wild, because the spikelets of wild grain are so brittle when ripe that as soon as they are touched they would break open. Therefore if the grain was cut with sickles, it must have been cultivated. Then too, the carefully carved sickle handles and the well-made querns and storage pits showed that the grain must have been very important to the Natufians and couldn't have been wild.

Others said there was no proof—that the storage pits might have been used for other things, that the sickles might have been used to cut reeds, and that the Natufians were nomadic hunters who may have come back to the same places from year to year when the wild wheat was ripe, and gathered it for the winter. It seems that they must have been coming back for a very long time, however. There were many feet of deposits in the caves, and on Mount Carmel they had done a good deal of construction. On the terrace in front of the cave they had put two lines of stones for some purpose. There were rings of stones that looked like fireplaces. And there were burials inside the cave and on the terrace.

For some years this was all that was known of the Natufians. And then suddenly more evidence appeared.

In the 1950's Dr. Kathleen Kenyon was working in Palestine, at the great mound called Tell-es-Sultan, which covers the ancient city of Jericho. Archaeologists had been digging there for more than fifty years, looking for the remains of the Biblical city whose walls came tumbling down when Joshua blew the trumpets. They had found the ruins of many towns, one below another, beside a perennial spring which gushes up from some unknown underground source. They knew it was a very old settlement, but they did not know how old until, in 1957, Dr. Kenyon's expedition dug all the way down to bed rock, and found Natufian flint tools on a rough plastered floor. In the floor were storage pits and stone querns. There were even the remains of an ancient shrine. The Natufian hunters had camped here beside the spring 11,000 years ago, and had built the first houses. From this beginning the city finally rose. It was here in the Jordan Valley that they had their start, and not in the caves, after all.

After that, Natufian tools and burials and houses were found at one site after another. They had settled all over Palestine, up and down the valley. Where there were caves, they lived in them. Otherwise they lived in the open, and built shelters. They usually lived near marshes and water, where fishing and hunting were good, for these provided most of their food. At Eynan, zoologists found bones of cattle, deer, gazelle, goat, wild pig, fox and rabbit, as well as many birds and fish, turtles and snails. From the caves came bear and leopard, deer and horse bones.

There were fishhooks and harpoons, carved of bone and without barbs, like the ones found at Fayum. Their stone tools were well made. There were chisels and carvers for cutting wood and bone. There were stones with notches or holes,

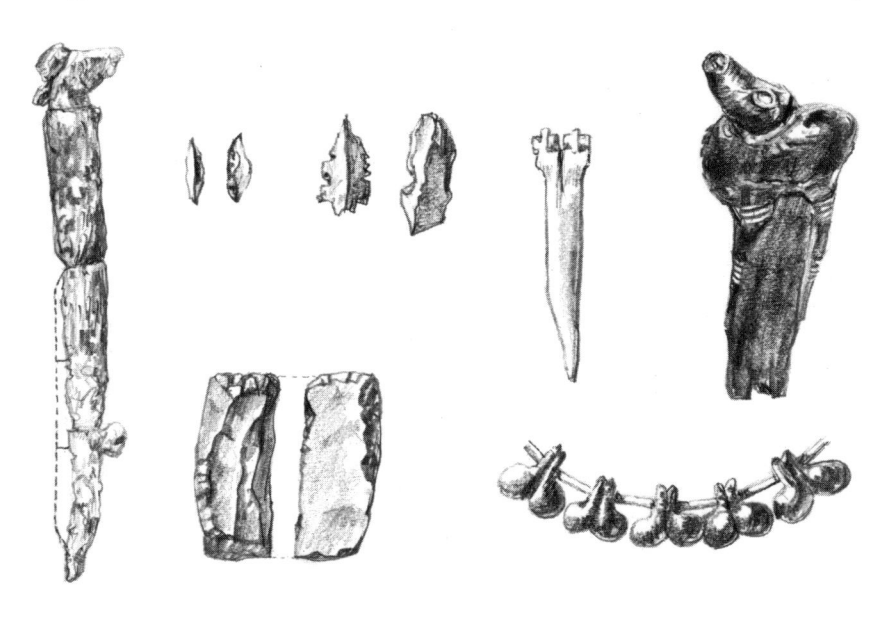

Natufian objects: sickle handles with animal heads; chipped flint sickle blades and points; bone point; necklace made of carved bones.

sinkers for fishing lines or nets. There were grooved stones for polishing bone, and bowls, mortars, pestles and beakers. And always, many querns, grinders and sickles.

At Eynan there were traces of clusters of circular houses, with storage pits around them. The houses had foundations of stone, with hearths sunk into the floors, and were probably covered with reeds from the lake.

In the floors and in some of the storage pits were graves. Sometimes a baby's grave would be made under a stone slab in the floor, as if the family wanted to keep the baby with them. Sometimes there were necklaces and headdresses made of dentalia shells from the Mediterranean shore not far away. Sometimes the skeletons were sprinkled with red ochre, which is iron ore, and palettes were found on which the ochre had been ground to powder. The use of red dye in burials is very ancient. It was used by Palaeolithic man fifty thousand years ago. Perhaps he thought that by using earth the color of blood, he could bring life back to the corpse.

At Eynan the tomb of an important person, perhaps a chieftain, was found inside a circular house. The tomb was a circle of stones, plastered and painted red, and it contained two skeletons. One, a man, was propped up on stones, facing the mountains. The other, perhaps a woman, wore a headdress of dentalia shells. It seems quite clear that these people, 10,000 years ago, had very definite beliefs about death, and probably about life after death.

We don't know what their beliefs were. We don't know what their speech was like, or their music, or their dancing.

But we know from their skeletons what they may have looked like. They were short sturdy people, about five feet tall, of Eurafrican or Mediterranean type, rather like the Egyptians found at Badari. They were artistic, and skilled at carving and decorating their tools and dishes. They were not yet Neolithic, for they had no domestic animals and there is no trace of any of their vegetable foods. But though they were still hunters and fishers and collectors, they were on the way to something else.

Recently, still more Natufian sites have been found, outside of Palestine, in the mountain slopes of Syria, Turkey, Lebanon and Iran. It seems that these people had spread over the entire area. Their villages are under the soil like an underground reservoir waiting to be tapped.

At Karim Shahir, on a hilltop in northeastern Iraq, there was a settlement of about three acres, with bones of animals that could have been domesticated, but probably were not. At Zawi Chemi, nearby, with a Carbon 14 date of about 8900 B.C. ± 300, there were bones of sheep that did appear to be domesticated. This place seems to have been occupied only half the year, and there is a cave nearby, called Shanidar, where the people probably lived during bad weather.

As in later cultures there were signs of trade and travel, for bitumen, or pitch made from petroleum, which must come from a hundred miles to the south, was used to fix sickle blades in place. And there was obsidian, which came from Lake Van in the north. There were luxury goods too—beads and pendants, rings and bracelets of beautiful stone, some even of copper. With trade, ideas must have spread, even in those early days.

Earlier still, at Belt Cave near the Caspian Sea, and at Zarzi in the Zagros Mountains, there were people who were hunters and fishermen, but who left flint tools and bones of goats similar to those at Shanidar. It is possible that they wandered down from the north. At Belbasi and Beldibi, on the Mediterranean coast of Turkey, there were Mesolithic people who left fine microliths, as well as rock paintings and drawings not unlike the Upper Palaeolithic of Europe.

So we come full circle, back to the type of Stone Age hunters whom we first met in the caves of France. These must all have been people on the eve of that great invention, still depending on wild food, but almost ready for a new way of life.

8 ❧ The Great Change Begins

We have come to a place and a time in which farming had its beginnings. It was not the only place and time in the world. Farming began in other places, for example North America where the Indians discovered how to raise corn.

But its beginning in the Near East was the oldest, and the one that most affected Western culture.

Here, in the hills of Southwest Asia, 10,000 years ago, something happened to start people living in a new way. It was so new that it has been called the Neolithic Revolution. We don't call it that so much any more. When we say "revolution" we mean a complete and quick change, and this change didn't happen overnight. Maybe the people didn't even realize that they were changing their way of life. It was more of a gradual drift into other ways of living.

Let us see if we can understand why this happened. The period we are discussing was a time of great change and disturbance over a large part of the planet. First there were great climatic changes. Always when climate changes, life changes.

One sort of animal moves out, another moves in. One form of plant dies, another form takes its place.

If a watcher from outer space could have looked through a powerful lens, he would have seen the white cap of ice that covered such a large part of the Northern Hemisphere start to shrink. At its edges he would have seen first the glitter of Arctic lakes and rivers, and then a veil of green, as forests grew up and covered the land.

The mammoth and the woolly rhinoceros followed the ice northward and finally died out. In the tundra, the treeless plain at the edge of the ice, herds of reindeer migrated, eating moss and flowers.

In the forests, new kinds of animals lived, deer and wolves and foxes.

The lakes and marshes teemed with fish. The seacoasts, rising from the newly melted waters of the seas, were full of shellfish.

The Palaeolithic hunters, men of the Old Stone Age, had to adapt to the new conditions. Some chose to follow the ice northward, and to continue living as the Eskimos do today. Some followed the herds of reindeer, living with them and on them, using their meat and milk and hides as the nomadic Lapps still do.

Those who stayed in the region of changing climate had to hunt the smaller and swifter animals, and to catch fish and water animals—beaver, seals and otters. They needed new kinds of weapons: bows and arrows, harpoons, spears and fishhooks. They needed new tools for working wood, a new material. They needed baskets and nets for the fish and shellfish and vegetables foods they gathered—acorns, berries, seeds, nuts, green plants and roots.

They still used stone tools, but a different kind—the tiny sharp flints we call microliths, set in bone or wood handles. These were the tools of the Mesolithic, the Middle Stone Age. They were found first in Europe—in France, then in the Swiss lake villages, then in the peat bogs of Denmark, and then in the Mediterranean countries—because Europe was where archaeology began. It now seems that they must have originated in the Near East and spread westward.

When the people of the northern lands found the climate changing, they certainly adapted to the new conditions. But they did not basically change their way of life. They were still hunters, fishermen and food-collectors. They simply hunted and collected more intensively, using every kind of food. It has been said they changed just enough so they would not have to change.

In the Near East it was different. There the climate did not change very much from what it had been. The Near East had never had the terrible weather of the Ice Age. Though there were some glaciers in the highest mountains, there had never been centuries of mile-thick ice covering the land. In fact, 10,000 years ago, the climate was not very different there from what it is today. The forests were thicker, and in the plains were grasslands where there are now deserts. There may have been more rain.

Certainly in the valleys and the mountain slopes, there was plenty of rain. There were also the other ingredients needed for the great change. In these hills were wild sheep and goats, cattle and pigs, animals that could be tamed. Here too were wild plants that could be domesticated.

These things had been here for a long time, and also for a long time there had been people coming regularly, when it was time to harvest the wild grain, and then going back to their regular hunting grounds. When the hunting grounds changed, they began to settle down in their camping places, and to take those animals and plants and adapt them for their own use, as they shaped bits of flint into knives, or stone into bowls. In the end the animals and plants would be creations of man, just as the tools and the bowls were.

We would like to know how this process began. We have little evidence, for those people left no writing. They left only their bones, and a few tools, and here and there a mudbrick wall or the mark of some reed matting in the dust.

But we have ways of guessing, for after all they were human beings, and we know what human beings are like. We have clues.

There are still a few groups of people living today who are remnants of the Stone Age. Such people are the Bushmen of the Kalahari Desert in South Africa. There are tribes of aborigines in central Australia; the Yukaghis, who hunt and fish in northern Siberia; the Semang of Malaya and others who live in the rain forests of Africa and Southeast Asia. There are Indians in the jungles of South America, and the hunter-fishers of Patagonia on the Chilean coast. And of course there are the Eskimos. All these people live in out-of-the-way places, or places so cold or wet or dry that nobody else wants them. They are still living pretty much as their ancestors did 10,000 or even 50,000 years ago.

There were many more of these Stone Age people in the seventeenth, eighteenth and nineteenth centuries. But in those days the explorers and colonists were so busy settling newly discovered places that they had no use for the primitive natives, except sometimes to use them as slaves. They thought them little better than animals.

It wasn't till the twentieth century that scientists suddenly realized that those aborigines had been preserving a model of the prehistory of mankind, and that they should be protected and studied before they died out, or became modern. These scientists who study the customs of living humans are anthropologists.

Luckily travelers had kept journals, and from those records, and from the living Stone Age people, anthropologists have deduced a lot about life before the beginning of cultivation and animal husbandry. They have made some guesses about how these things started. All those people have two main ways of getting food. One is hunting, which is done mostly by men. The other, just as important, is the steady, daily collecting done by the women and children. They go out each day with their bags and digging sticks. They collect everything edible —and things we wouldn't consider edible: insects, toads, lizards, snails; many kinds of vegetable food—roots, leaves, flowers, seeds, fruits.

An Australian tribe used seventy-three different plants, some for their roots, some grasses for their seeds, shrubs and trees for their fruit. Many of these were ground up into paste, made into cakes or porridge, and baked or boiled.

Such people know a great deal about plants. They know

Bushman woman grinding food.

which are safe to eat raw, and which must be cooked, and which are poisonous. When Captain Cook visited Australia in 1770, his men got very sick from eating a certain fruit which the natives ate. He concluded that the natives must have some way of treating it to make it harmless. Sure enough, a later traveler tells what the women do. They soak the fruit in water, then bury it in sand for a couple of weeks, and finally dig it up and remove the kernels. The pulp is then fit to eat.

Bushman hunting.

These people know about the habits of plants—where they grow, when they ripen.

One Australian tribe ate lots of yams and other roots. The women knew when each kind was ripe, and the tribe made its visits to the places where they grew at those times.

Another tribe did a sort of planting. They found that when peeling their yams, if they threw the skins and tops into black soil, they would find a good patch of yams there the next year.

From knowing how a plant grows, it is just a step to knowing how to take care of it. This same tribe had a law that no seed-bearing plant was to be dug up after it had bloomed. The plant was allowed to set seed, and was called the "mother" of the species.

Taking care of plants does not mean gardening, exactly, for gardening involves many jobs—digging the soil, planting, pruning, protecting the plants, weeding, fertilizing and sometimes watering. The women may do one or another of these things, but not all of them.

For instance, the Semang tribe of the Malay Peninsula will cut away the bushes from under their wild fruit trees, and chop off excess branches. The purpose is to make it easier to reach the fruit, but the pruning also benefits the trees. Some of these people even plant seeds of their trees, and their ownership is respected by others.

The Bushmen of the Kalahari depend mostly on hunting,

but their women also collect every kind of vegetable and small animal they can find. Just before the wet season, they burn the dry grass. This not only drives the game into the open, but is a kind of cultivation as it makes the bulbs and roots taste better, and improves the new grass, which attracts animals.

There are interesting stories of the Indians of North America. Of course many of them were skilled farmers before Europeans ever saw them. But others were still gatherers. The Assiniboine Indians of western Canada, for instance, used to depend on the wild rice that grew in the lakes. They sowed it in the marshes, and came back later when it was ripe, to gather it. The Ojibwa Indians of Wisconsin also liked the wild rice, but they did not plant it. However, they weeded out the grass between the rice stalks, and respected each other's property rights to certain areas.

In British Columbia, the Indians lived on dry salmon all winter. This got pretty tiresome, and they liked a nice dish of greens with their fish in the spring when the sweet clover and skunk cabbage came up. When a woman found a patch of either one growing, she would weed it, put a fence around it, and drive away the deer, but never seemed to think of trying to plant any herself.

The Paiute Indians of California did none of these things, but they liked tender, young pig-weed, and when they found some growing, they would take the trouble to irrigate it.

They built dams to collect snow water. When the weather got dry, they would poke holes in the dams, let some water run out, and then stop up the holes with clay.

But one of the most interesting of these old-fashioned people is a tribe of reindeer hunters, the Chukchi, in northeastern Asia. They don't practice agriculture, but they always have a mixture of plants growing around their huts. The plants have grown up from seeds the people bring home and drop on the ground, and they grow luxuriously in the rich soil around the houses. They become the household plants of the families, and form an important part of their diet. Some plant scientists think this is the oldest form of gardening in the world.

The women who do all this don't think of themselves as gardeners. These are just things they are in the habit of doing. Actually, all of these are examples of people and plants living together, what we call symbiosis. Plants and man share the same living space; the people use the plants, get to know them, take care of them, and soon the plants begin to show the effects. A woman digs holes in the soil to get roots, and lays bare a place where seeds can sprout. The wind, or an animal, carries some seeds there, and suddenly there is a patch of pig-weed or clover that wasn't there before. Or a woman brings home a basket full of plants, and unknowingly drops some seeds on the ground in front of the door. Pretty soon she has a collection of all kinds of plants growing around the house. She can go out and pick her dinner from her wild garden. Or she may weed out the things she doesn't want there, and thus give the remaining plants a better chance.

The same sort of symbiosis must have existed between man and animals. People living close to animals understand their ways and like them. Even the hunter likes and sympathizes with the animals he kills. The American Indians, when they had killed a bear or a deer, would carry out a very important ceremony before eating the meat. They would thank the spirit of the animal for allowing itself to be caught, and would apologize for killing it, explaining that this was necessary. This was insurance that the spirit would allow itself to be caught another time.

If a hunter killed a mother animal, he might bring home her helpless baby, and the women and children might raise it as a pet. Of course if it was a baby bear or a lion cub, it might run away or be killed when it grew bigger, but a wild lamb or kid or dog would be likely to grow up tame and stay with its human family.

In Australia today, the natives will bring home little opossums or kangaroos, birds or rats, and keep them tied up around the camp. They like to make pets of the dingo dogs, the wild dogs of that part of the world, but they don't breed them. Instead the men bring home wild puppies, and the women raise them like babies.

Probably Mesolithic people behaved the same way, since

it seems that people everywhere like pets. Of course pet-keeping could not have been the beginning of all domestication. But it must surely have played a part in the taming of dogs, for dogs were man's first companions. Dog bones are found in the oldest deposits of the Near East and Europe.

Wild dogs, jackals and the smaller wolves, are scavengers, and they probably hung around the hunters' campfires waiting to be thrown a bone or to clean up after a meal.

In this way they must have gotten used to following men about. Then, since dogs like to run in packs and follow a leader, they might be willing to leave the pack and follow man as a leader in the hunt. It would not be long before the man learned that the dog's sensitive nose was a great help, and from then on the two were partners.

But what about the other domestic animals? It happens that goats, sheep, cattle, horses, even camels are all social animals, used to running in herds. Herds can be driven.

Palaeolithic man knew how to drive them. He often drove herds of horses or bison over a cliff, to get a quick supply of meat.

It also happens that wolves, and their relatives the dogs, know how to drive herds. It is possible to see a wolf even today, in the northern tundra, driving a herd of reindeer in order to cut one out for its dinner. Probably Mesolithic man discovered this, and then man and dog were partners in herding reindeer, wild sheep and goats.

It may be that in the Zagros Mountains, 10,000 years ago, nomadic hunters and their dogs rounded up a few sheep or goats to be penned up near camp as a meat supply, while they waited for the wild wheat or barley to ripen.

Probably, as the years passed, goat- and sheep-keeping became a custom. As wheat seeds dropped around the camp, first by chance and then purposely, became an important possession, it was necessary to stay near the fields to protect them, instead of going off on hunting trips. For as the gardens got bigger, the crop robbers came—the cattle and pigs, attracted by the delicious food.

This might have been a disaster at first, for the wild cattle and boars were large and fierce and dangerous. But if some of them could be killed, there would be meat for the whole tribe. And if some young ones could be caught, they could be kept prisoner, now that there was surplus food to give them.

The zoologists say that it is hard to tell, from the animal bones, which were wild and which were domesticated, for in the early days they were very much alike. One clue which is easier to pinpoint is age. It is easier to recognize the bones of very young animals. Since hunters don't usually kill very young animals, and villagers do, it is thought that a large number of juvenile bones shows early domestication.

So the tribe, which was now a village, began to keep cattle and pigs. Calves and piglets born in captivity would be quite tame, and could even be used as decoys to catch more wild creatures. There would be food for them, and extra milk for baby animals and humans.

As the village grew, other crops would be planted—peas and lentils and apples and peaches. As more land was needed, the people might decide to move down from the mountain slopes to the plains below.

Then some sort of irrigation system would have to be devised, for there was not as much rain down below. This would mean community action.

And then someone would invent a plow to take the place of the old digging stick. At first a man or a couple of women would pull it, but then someone would discover that if cattle were docile enough, their great strength could be used to pull not only a plow but a sledge and later a cart with wheels.

Still later, other animals would be domesticated in other places—the horse in Persia, the donkey in Egypt, the zebu in India, not to mention camels, yaks, water buffaloes, reindeer and poultry.

The process is still going on. In Kenya, Africa, some people are trying to domesticate elands, the large antelopes of the plains; and in Alaska musk oxen are being bred, in the hope that these large cattle, with hairy skirts like dust ruffles, will provide meat for the Eskimos.

But the main work was done long ago.

9 ᛫ Animals and Plants Change

We have seen how, in looking for the first farmers, archaeologists have been helped by other scientists.

Botanists have identified plant remains. Zoologists have studied animal bones. Anthropologists have studied living humans and made deductions about the behavior of long-dead ones.

All these have helped explain what must have happened to plants, animals and people to make agriculture possible. But why should it have happened at all? That is, why was it possible?

Just keeping animals penned up doesn't mean they are domesticated. And just planting seeds doesn't mean you have cultivated plants. Something more has to happen. That something is a gradual change in the animals and plants, a change that does not take place in the wild, but does take place when people take animals and plants out of their natural habitat.

Another science has to help us understand this phenomenon—the science of genetics, the study of heredity.

In nature, living things have to compete for life. Nature produces many more of each kind than there is room or food for. We don't say that nature has a purpose, but the result is obvious. Only the best of each species will live to grow up. The others die, providing food for the survivors, either by being eaten or by fertilizing the soil. This is called the survival of the fittest.

Big fish eat little fish, and only the fastest get away. Foxes eat baby rabbits, and only the best camouflaged escape. In a herd of wild goats, the best jumpers and climbers get the most food from the shrubs on the hillsides, and also have the best chance of getting away from wolves. The amount of wild food is limited, and the goats that don't get enough are weak, and are caught by the wolves.

The best fighters among the males, those with the biggest horns, protect the herd from wolves, and win the most attractive females, by driving off the other males.

All this sounds cruel, but it is the natural way of keeping the herd in good condition. It is part of the struggle for existence.

But good climbers and fighters don't make the best domestic goats. Thin muscular animals don't make the best eating. Their meat is tough. Big horns are dangerous. A herdsman would be glad to see these things changed.

When the Mesolithic hunters penned up a few adult goats or sheep, these animals might become somewhat tame. That is, they would get used to being with people, and would accept food from them. They were still wild enough, however, to escape at the first chance and run with their wild relatives. They would breed with them, and the babies would be like their wild ancestors, finding their own food and protecting themselves against enemies. Physically, they would not be changed at all.

When the hunters brought home a baby kid or lamb, it might become a pet. It might even think the woman who fed it was its mother.

Such a little goat would be quite tame, and perhaps would not want to play with other goats. But in appearance it would still be a wild goat.

But later on, the hunters, who were now becoming herdsmen, might have larger numbers of goats or sheep. They would keep them fenced in so they couldn't breed with their wild relatives. They would feed the animals—drive them to pasture, or give them some of the garden surplus. This would not mean they grew big or fat. The domestic animals of primitive men are not well fed. They tend to be smaller and weaker than their wild relatives at first, which would make them easier to manage. And the hunter herdsmen would make a point of getting rid of any animals that were too unruly. They would keep only the most docile and tame ones, and the fighters and jumpers would end up in the soup pot.

Then when these penned up animals had babies, something would happen that could not happen in nature. The babies that were weak and small and couldn't jump the fence, instead of dying out, would be kept alive by men. They would be protected against wolves, so that they didn't need big horns or long legs.

And as time went on and the herd animals continued to breed, these characteristics, which are desirable in tame animals but not in wild ones, would be exaggerated.

Why does this happen? Because in the reproductive cells of the animals there are tiny particles called genes, which are passed on from parent to child and cause the traits of the parents to appear in the child. That is why children look like their parents. There are tens of thousands of these microscopic genes, and there are many traits. Some of them are strong, or dominant. They come out in most offspring. For instance,

Wild mountain goat.

in some families, most of the children have dark hair and eyes. But some traits are recessive, like green eyes. They appear in only a few children.

In goats, some of these recessive traits, like small horns, or short legs, or black and white coats, were the very ones that the herdsmen wanted. Of course the herdsmen didn't know anything about genes. They did find out gradually that they could control the kind of animals they had by allowing certain ones to breed, and killing off the others.

And it happened that certain traits went together. For instance, if a sheep has genes that make it docile and mild, it will also usually have the genes for a broad skull, short horns, short legs, smaller teeth and jaws, and more fat. Such an animal would make better eating, wouldn't run much, and could be more manageable. At the same time it would also be

Domestic sheep.

more dependent on humans and less able to take care of itself.

So the human herders found out what kind of animals they wanted and how to control their reproduction. They would keep the quieter ones, the best milkers, the largest and most fleshy, the ones with the softest wool and the nicest colors. They would kill off the wild relatives which might spoil the flock and tempt the tame ones to run away. They would drive their herds to other climates and make them adapt to other foods.

And after a while they would have a quite new kind of animal, entirely dependent on man for protection and food, in other words, domesticated.

Of course some of the wild traits might still be hidden in the genes of the domesticated animals. Now and then they appear. A perfectly tame, well-behaved cow may have a little bull calf who is more lively and fierce than his brothers. He jumps about, butting everybody and causing trouble. The farmer may send him off to be made into steaks. Or he may keep him for breeding because he is strong, and that will be good for the herd. In Spain, he might be sent to the bull ring.

Or there may be a dog who catches chickens, or a goat that keeps running away. If man disappeared, these animals would survive while the others would probably die for lack of food. The race might then revert to the wild.

As for plants, in some ways the same things happen. In other ways it is more complicated because there are more of them. In nature, the tendency is to blanket the earth with a plant cover. Incredible numbers of seeds are scattered each year. Millions of them are eaten by birds or other animals, or dry up, or rot, or perhaps die after sprouting. There is a constant struggle for space, water, sun and nourishment. The ones that succeed in growing into mature plants are the ones with the best traits for survival. But those aren't necessarily the best for domestication.

Up on the mountain slopes, in the prehistoric Near East, wild grasses grew, wild wheat and barley, all mixed together. The heads of the wild grain, or spikes, consisted of a stalk, called a rachis, holding a number of little spikelets. (Rachis comes from a Greek word meaning spine.) Each spikelet held one or more seeds. Each seed was tightly wrapped in a little sheath called a glume, and had a stiff little hair sticking out called an awn. The glume was to protect the seed and keep it from sprouting too soon after falling to earth. For if it sprouted at once it might die before the next rain. The bristly little awn helped make the grain unpleasant for animals to eat. When the grain was ripe, the rachis would break apart and the spikelets would scatter far and wide.

Suppose some women went to the valley to gather the grain. They might have to be careful to catch the seeds before they fell to the earth. Or they might even have to reap it while it was still a little green, to keep it from scattering. This is a nuisance.

But in a field full of wild grain there are usually some plants with recessive traits. Among them are some with tough rachises that don't break up when ripe. They are much easier to reap. You just take the stem in one hand and cut with the other. If you were going to take home some seeds to plant, these would be just the kind to take.

The tough rachis would be a recessive trait, because in nature this is the kind that would not survive. The seeds would not fall to the ground in time, or if they did, they would not scatter far enough from the parent plant. But if a woman plants them, she will take care that they are properly scattered and planted at the right time. When the grains form and release their pollen, these plants will be cross-bred so as to bring out the recessive trait still more, and by and by all of the grain in the garden will be of this tough-rachis type, entirely dependent on the hand of man (or woman) for its life.

Then some other recessive traits may come out. Some of the grain may be beardless, and some may be naked, without glumes or hulls. This makes it much easier to thresh.

Then perhaps the tribe wants to plant a bigger field. So they move down the mountain to the plain. Here the climate is warmer and drier. Now wheat and barley were originally high-altitude plants. They were adapted to cold weather and lots of rain. Down in the plain, other recessive traits come out which would not have survived on the mountain. Perhaps the heads get bigger and heavier. The barley grows in six-row heads instead of two-row.

By this time the idea of cultivation has spread to include other plants, and things happen to them too.

Those that have thorns, or a bitter taste, or poisonous roots, lose these traits through breeding. They become more useful

Above: Wild wheat/Wild wheat shattering when ripe.
Below: Two types of cultivated wheat, one drawn to show individual kernels.

to man, but they also lose their natural protection and become dependent. The wild fruits lose their large seeds and become more fleshy. The wild cabbage develops a large head. There are fewer individual plants or fruits, but the harvest is better because each one is fleshier and less space is taken by seeds.

Sometimes the new trait comes from a gene in one plant. Then it is called a mutant. Sometimes it is the result of cross-pollination. This is called a hybrid.

Little by little, farmers have learned to develop the kind of hybrids they wanted. They have bred plants that could resist disease or drought, plants that would ripen all at one time instead of a few at a time, plants that would cover the ground so that weeds could not grow, plants with beautiful leaves or flowers or fruits, plants with no seeds, that have to be reproduced from cuttings. Eventually they developed new kinds which had never been seen before, and which, like the domestic animals, are the creations of man.

10 ⚜ People Change

This has been like a story of a game of hare and hounds. The hares have left, not bits of paper, but clues buried in the earth. The hounds, coming along thousands of years later, cannot catch up with the hares, but know where they have been. They have traced them back to their settlements in the hills above the Fertile Crescent and seen how the new way of life spread.

As there was more food, the population grew. As it grew, it had to expand. People began migrating, looking for new land. They took with them their tools and seeds and animals. The great invention spread with them.

It went east, to India and Southeast Asia. At least, the idea went. We are not sure about the first cultivated crops there, for the damp heat of the tropics has destroyed the evidence. The native grain there is rice, the native animals pigs and chickens. These, with millet, sorghum and soy beans, were cultivated in China about 3500 B.C. So perhaps the idea spread from India to China.

The great invention went west, along the shores of the Mediterranean to Turkey, Cyprus, Palestine.

We know how Abraham moved to Palestine with his herds and his tribe. We know how Jericho grew from a simple Natufian camping place into a walled and fortified city. We know that in 6000 B.C. there were farming villages in Syria, and that in Turkey at this time people were living in mud-brick houses with painted walls, and using pottery decorated with stylized human heads, like our present-day Toby jugs.

About this time agriculture spread to Europe. On the plain of Macedonia in northern Greece, there was a lake about 6,000 years ago. Along its shores lived farmers who raised grain and kept goats and sheep. They hunted and fished too, and gathered shellfish from the lake. Some of their pots were decorated with faces like those from Hassuna, and from Hacilar in Turkey. There were clay stamps and bone belt hooks like some found in Turkey, and white stone ear studs like those from Jarmo in Iraq and Tepe Siyalk in Iran. Either this was a sign of trade, or it meant that the people had come from the East and brought their styles with them.

The new way of life spread to Egypt. In 4300 B.C., nearly 1,500 years after Hassuna, there were villages like Hassuna in the Fayum, and others at Khartoum in the Sudan a thousand years later.

The trend was westward. When the land was exhausted, the people packed their belongings on the backs of their donkeys, or on sledges, and started out, driving the goats and sheep before them. They would move a few miles, settle down and build houses, and plant their fields. Perhaps twenty years later they would move again.

As people spread, their ideas spread. Perhaps at first the natives stared suspiciously at the newcomers. Then they began to imitate them. Maybe they took away their crops and livestock by force. Maybe they married into the new tribe. Maybe visitors and traders came, and went away taking seeds or a young kid, or a wife who knew the art of planting.

The farmers of Europe made their own adjustments. They had their own style of building and tool-making. They domesticated the native plants of Europe—apples and pears, rye and oats. The imported animals and plants adapted to the new climate, altitude and soil.

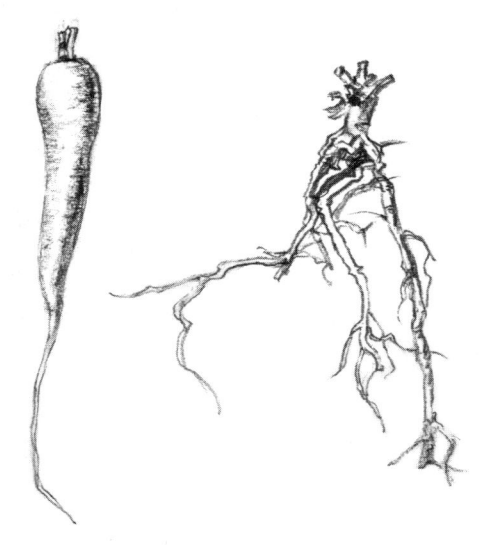

Roots of carrot: cultivated and wild.

While the pioneers were pushing into the wilderness, back in Mesopotamia great city states had grown up. Writing was perfected, sculpture and architecture developed into arts. About 3500 B.C. the wheel was invented. Civilization arrived.

Little by little, this too would spread across Europe, until at last the colonists would cross the ocean. There they would find Stone Age men whose ancestors had arrived by the back door, so to speak, through Alaska, and had invented agriculture independently, in their own way.

And so one species, the human race, has taken over and settled the entire world. In a brief 10,000 years, people have changed not only the domestic animals and plants, but the wild ones too.

For wild animals are driven out when man takes over the land. Or they learn to adjust to man, by living with him or stealing from him. Wild plants die out, or become weeds which spring up wherever farmers lay bare the soil.

Changes take place in the earth itself, as man interferes with it. As long as man lived the life of a wandering hunter, he did not disturb nature very much, though he might accidentally set a forest on fire, or wipe out herds of horses by driving them over cliffs. But when farmers began to cut down trees to make fields, and to let their goats and sheep eat up all the grass and shrubs in a pasture, the natural balance was upset. The result might often be drought and dust storms, or floods which washed away the soil, or deserts.

In the modern world, people interfere even more with their surroundings. They use up the underground water supply, they use chemicals which kill birds and fish, they fill the air with unnatural gases and cover the ground with concrete.

On the credit side, they have made the deserts bloom, replanted forests and rebuilt soil.

But the greatest changes are in the humans themselves. Physically, people aren't very different from the men and women of Jericho and Badari. Some are bigger, but others haven't changed. No. The important human changes result from one thing: the number of people who are able to remain alive.

Before the days of farming, probably only the strongest survived. The aged, the sick, the weak died, as they do among the Eskimos. There was no food to spare for anybody who could not do his share toward getting it. But as the food supply became more reliable, and people stayed put, more of the weaker children stayed alive.

And the children were useful. To farmers, extra hands meant better harvests. Then, too, in the village there was a place for those with a talent for painting and carving, and the village could afford to let craftsmen spend their time at their crafts. That is the meaning of the jewelry, carvings and painted pottery the villagers left.

The greatest change came when people began living in

cities. When many people live and work together, they stimulate each other. One person gets an idea, and other people hear of it and improve on it. Ideas accumulate and form a pool of knowledge. Invention, religion, literature are built up.

As Mesopotamian cities grew, people were freed by agriculture to become artists, engineers, soldiers or priests.

But not all people were freed. Some people had to work in the fields to produce the food the others needed. Those were the farmers. When the great civilizations arose, there had to be big farms, and many farmers. That meant a big change from the little farming village where each man was independent. It meant a farming class, a class of peasants.

In Sumer, for the first time, there were separate classes of people. The peasants were far down in the scale. For them, life was hard, and remained so for a long time.

There were other unpleasant things that resulted from civilization. There was war. And there was disease.

Of course they existed before, but with the coming of civilization they increased. As wealth piled up, there was more to fight for. Kings made war on their neighbors, to snatch away not only treasure but also slaves to work in their fields and mines. And as people lived crowded in cities, disease spread.

But there was also law and the search for peace and justice. There was science, which wiped out plagues so that more people might remain alive. And right there, it is important to stop and think.

How many people are going to remain alive?

There was a time when we would have said, the more the better. Didn't Jehovah say, "Be fruitful, and multiply, and replenish the earth, and subdue it?"

It made sense in Bible days, and even as recently as a couple of hundred years ago. When the only kind of power was human muscle power, when a farmer needed many sons to till his fields, when factories needed many hands to run the machines, and when many babies died of childhood diseases, it made sense to have as many children as possible. People didn't live to be very old either, as a rule.

Now it appears that this picture has changed. A new group of scientists, the demographers, who study populations, say there is a great danger of too many people being alive at one time.

There are three billion on earth now, they say, and every day that passes there are 120,000 more. By the year 2000 there will be six billion people, if nothing happens to stop the trend.

This isn't just because so many more are being born, though that is a big factor. It is also because so many don't die. We have learned to save babies so they can live to grow up. We save grownups so they live to be old. And this is fine, only the demographers say there isn't enough food for them all now, and in ten or fifteen years it will be even worse.

Not enough food? Don't we have all we can eat? Yes, in the United States and Canada and the other developed nations. But in Asia, Africa and Latin America, we are told, three out of four people don't have enough to eat, or don't have the right things. Many people in Asia live on nothing but rice. They need fats and proteins (meat, eggs, fish) but they don't get them. They tell us that in some of those countries 42 per cent (nearly half) of the people are under fifteen. That means that millions of children are growing up without the milk and eggs and hamburgers and vitamins that they need for their bodies and minds to grow properly. And thousands are actually starving.

What is to be done?

Many things are being done. The developed nations are sending food and money to the hungry countries. They are sending advisers to teach better methods of farming; sending better seeds, and fertilizer, and farm machinery to step up the production.

Chemists are trying to find new sources of food—from the sea, from the earth, from the air. Some say we will have to eat food raised on petroleum, or made from concentrated plankton. We wonder how it will taste.

Other scientists are developing ways of farming additional

land, taking the salt out of sea water to irrigate deserts, or learning how to raise food in the jungles.

Still others say that the only hope is to persuade people in the hungry nations to reduce their birth rate.

Some experts say that none of these remedies will work on a large enough scale to do much good. They say it is too late, that the problem is growing faster than the remedies. They say that even if new types of food could be produced in large quantities, it would take years to teach people to eat it. They say it is slow work to teach peasants who have been plowing their fields and cooking their food as their ancestors did 6,000 years ago to change to modern methods.

They say that people love children, and that it is a very slow and difficult task to persuade them to have small families, even in those countries where parents hear their children cry from hunger.

They say we are spending money and effort on war, which should be spent on solving our problems.

They say that we cannot avoid widespread famine in the next ten or twenty years, and with it, riot and disorder.

Other experts, who are working hard at all these jobs, say the situation is not quite so hopeless as that. In any case, we cannot just give way to despair.

There is a story about a lady who always said a little prayer when she was about to drive her automobile: "Lord, guide my hands to steer this car." But one day when she was in a bad traffic jam, she threw up her hands and said, "Lord, take the wheel."

We cannot afford to be like this lady and decide the problem is impossible to solve. People have done many impossible things. Fifty years ago, some people were saying that the world's supply of coal would soon be used up at the rate we were going, and that there would be no more fuel to run factories, steel mills, trains, or to heat homes. Today we have oil and atomic power. Perhaps the impossible task of feeding mankind will also be accomplished.

It would be interesting to know what the archaeologists of the future will find when they dig down to the level of the twentieth century. Among the pieces of plastic and metal and concrete, will they find signs of disorder and poverty? Or will they find the beginnings of the third or fourth or fifth greatest invention?

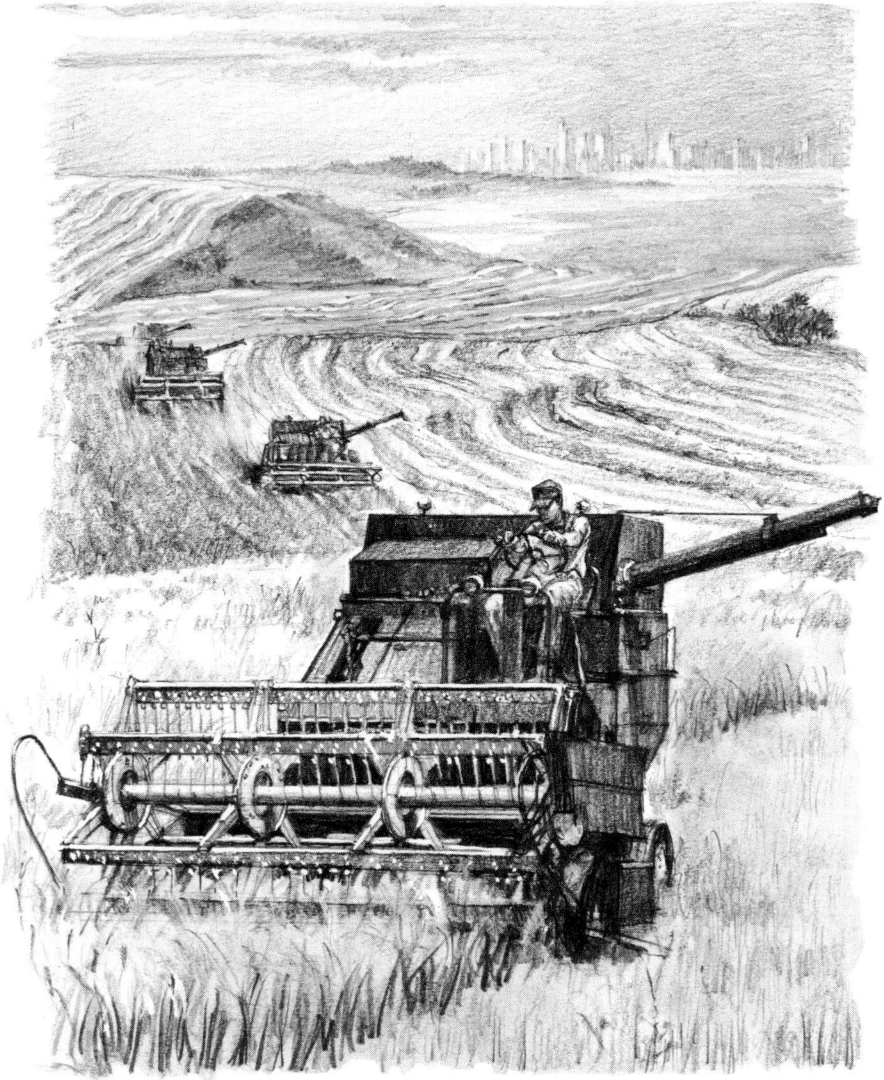

Index

Agriculture, 82, 83, 86–89, 92–93, 98–102
   See also farmers, food
Al 'Ubaid, 49
   pottery, 50
Animals
   domestication of, 82, 89–92, 94–98
   in Egypt, 35–38
   Ice Age, 9–11, 80, 82
   Mesolithic, 13, 80
   Natufian, 72, 75, 77
   Near East, 51, 57, 69
   Swiss lake villages, 20, 21
   See also individual sites
Archaeology, 5, 49, 55–56, *57*
Assyria, 40, *44,* 45, 46, 48, 49
Axes, stone, 12, 15, 18, 19, 33, 37, 66
   See also tools, weapons

Badari, 34
Barley, 20, 35, 36, 38, 68, 73, 99
   Bible, 2, 6, 26, 40, 46
Botta, Paul Émile, 42
Braidwood, Linda, 63
Braidwood, Dr. Robert, 63–65
Bronze Age, 11, 12, 18, 21
   See also dating

Carbon 14, 58–61, 66
Cave dwellings, 71–73, 77–78
Cuneiform writing, 44, 48

Dating, 31, 58–60
   Carbon 14, 58–61
   Jarmo, 66–67
   pollen, 58
   sequence-dating, 34, 36, 58
   varves, 58
Domestication of animals, 94–98
   See also animals

Earth, age of, 6
Egypt, 25–38, 42, 104
   domestic animals, 35, 36, 37, 38
   farming, 25, 35, 36
   food, 26, 35, 36
   graves, 28, 32
   hieroglyphics, 26–28
   houses, 33, 34, 35, 36
   Petrie, W. M. F., 30–33
   tools, 37–38

Farmers, 4, 21–24
   See also agriculture, Al 'Ubaid,

Note: All illustration references are in italics.

Egypt, Hassuna, Jarmo, Mesopotamia, Tell Halaf
Farming, *see* farmers
Fayum, the, 36, 104
Fertile Crescent, 61–62, 70, 103
Flint, *see* tools, stone
Flood, the, 6, 9, 46
Food, 4, 11, 103
   Bushmen, 84, 85
   collecting, 84
   in Egypt, 26, 35, 51
   in Mesolithic, 81
   in Near East, 69
   in Palaeolithic, 16, 17
   of Stone Age people today, 84–89
   in Swiss lake villages, 21–23

Genes, 96, 97, 102
Genetics, 93
Gerzeh, 33
Glaciers, 9, *10,* 12, 58
Goats, 38, 51, 61, 82, 94
Grain, 21, 33, 48 61, 68, 73, 99–101
Graves
   Egyptian, 28, *32,* 35, 36
   Natufian, 74, 76
   Neanderthal, 16

Halafian culture, 52–54
   pottery, 52
Hassuna, 60, 63, 70, 104
Hieroglyphics, 26–28
Houses
   in Egypt, 33–36, 38
   at Jarmo, *67*
   in Mesopotamia, 50, 51, 61
   Natufian, 76
   in Swiss lake villages, 19, *20*
Hunting, 15, 16, 17, 21, 24, 51, 70, 72, 80, 81, 84, 89, 90, 94

Iran, 39, 51, 70, 104
Iraq, 39, 52, 60, 104
Iron Age, 12, 22
   See also dating

Jarmo, 63–69, 104
   house foundations, 67
   site, 64

Kuyunjik, 42

Lake villages (Swiss)
   animals, 21
   grain, 21
   houses, 19, *20*
   implements, 18, 19, 21, 22, *23*
   pottery, 22
Layard, Austen Henry, 43–44, 55

Man, origin of, 2, 3, 9
   Cro-Magnon, 16, 17
   Neanderthal, 15, 17, 71
   Stone Age, 11
      See also Neolithic, Palaeolithic, Stone Age people today
Mariette, Auguste Édouard, 29
Merimde, 36
Mesolithic Age, 14, 81
Mesopotamia, 39, 46
   See also Iraq
Microliths, 71, 78, 81
Middle East, *see* Near East
Mount Carmel, 71, *72*

Nakada, 32
Natufians, 71–78

116

animal food, 75
burials, 74, 76
houses, 76
tools, *71–75*
vegetable food, 72–74
wild grain, 73
Near East, 39–54, 81
Neolithic man, 13, 21, 22, 33, 69
Neolithic Revolution, 79
Nineveh, 41, 44, 47, 54

Palaeolithic man, 13, 16, 24, 37, 75, 76, 78, 80
Palestine, 39
Persia, *see* Iran
Petrie, William Matthew Flinders, 30–34, 36, 38
Plant material as clue, 57
Plants
  domestication of, 82, 98
  collecting of, 84
  preparation of, 85
  care of, 86–88
Pottery
  Egyptian, 32–33, 35–36, 37–38
  in Europe, 104
  Halafian, 52
  Lake village, 22, *23,* 30
  in Mesopotamia, 49–50
  'Ubaidian, 50
  See also individual sites

Rawlinson, Henry Creswicke, 44–45

Sheep, 38, 51, 61, 82, 94, *96, 97*
Sickles, 35, *37,* 38, 51, 53, 72, 73, 75, 78
Stone Age, 11
  New, *see* Neolithic
  Old, *see* Palaeolithic
Stone Age people today, 82–89
Sumer, 46, 48, 49
Survival of the fittest, 94
Switzerland, 17–24
  See also lake villages

Tablets, clay, 41, 44, *45*
Tell Halaf, 52
Tells, *41,* 65
Thomsen, Christian Jurgensen, 12
Three-Age system, 12, 22
  See also dating
"Thunderbolts," *7,* 8
Tools, stone, *3, 7, 11, 13*
  chipped, 13
  flint, 63, 66
  polished or ground, 12, 13, 18, 35
  See also individual sites
Trade, 48, 53, 77–78, 105
Turkey, 70, 104

'Ubaidian culture, 50–52
  pottery, *50–53*
Ur, 40, 48, 49

Village sites, 19, 32–37, 56, 61, 66, 67, 70, 77
  See also individual sites

Wadi-en-Natuf, 71
Weapons, 11, 16, 22, 32, 33, 81
Wheat, 20, 35, 36, 37, 38 68, 73, 99, *101*
Woolley, Sir Leonard, 49

Zagros Mountains, 63, 68, 78, 91
ziggurats, *47,* 48

With over two hundred fruit trees on her family's country place as her inspiration, Eleanor Clymer decided as a very young girl that she wanted to be a farmer. She studied botany and zoology and continued her exploration into science throughout her college years at the University of Wisconsin. When she married and had a son, her interest turned from science to educational development and to writing books for children. She now has over thirty children's books to her credit. Many of her books like *The Big Pile of Dirt* and *My Brother Stevie,* an A.L.A. Notable Book, reflect the special needs and interests of children. Often, however, Mrs. Clymer turns to her earlier fascination with science, as in *Search for a Living Fossil* and now *The Second Greatest Invention.* Mrs. Clymer enjoys living in an old house in northern Westchester which she says is not actually a farm, but provides almost as much work as one, so that her childhood dream has in some measure been realized.

Lili Réthi was born in Vienna and educated there at the Academy of Art. In 1939, she came to live in New York City. The illustrator of over sixty-four books, Miss Réthi is especially well known for her drawings of industry and construction. Architecture, portrait, and historical material are among her other particular art interests. Her illustrations for *The Second Greatest Invention* reflect her fascination with the history of development, in this case the development of farming. She has had numerous one-man exhibits in Europe and the United States. In 1961, she was elected a Fellow of the Royal Society of Arts of London, in recognition of her work.

About the Book: The text is set in linotype Granjon; display type is French Oldstyle and Palatino Italic; the book was printed by offset. Lili Réthi illustrated the book with pencil drawings, getting a great range of values and textures from that medium.

J913.03 224863
Clymer
The second greatest invention.

DATE DUE

Johnson Free Public Library
Hackensack, New Jersey